OLIVE BRANCHES

A Hope for Peace for All Americans

by

Stan E. Hughes
aka Ha-Gue-A-Dees-Sas

DORRANCE PUBLISHING CO
EST. 1920
PITTSBURGH, PENNSYLVANIA 15238

Dorrance Publishing Co
585 Alpha Drive
Pittsburgh, PA 15238
Visit our website at *www.dorrancebookstore.com*

ISBN: 978-1-4809-8770-8
eISBN: 978-1-4809-8793-7

CONTENTS

DEDICATION

Olive Branches is dedicated to my six grandchildren, Coleman, Maev Rose, Benny, Aedyn, Sofia, Fiona, and my great granddaughter Saoirse. Each, in their own way, is peering through an open doorway toward the wonders of the world of today and in hope and expectation, wondering what lies ahead for them. I believe it is the responsibility of all of us to embrace children preparing to take those important steps and to guide them toward success.

This publication is also dedicated to the Peacemakers who face insurmountable odds as they endeavor to make things better for all of us.

And, of course, it is dedicated to Phyllis Betts, the heart of my heart and one of the most special people I have ever known.

INTRODUCTION

So … who is writing books about peace these days?

A look at Barnes & Noble Bookstore's "This Fall's 15 Biggest Books – Nonfiction" lists four titles with war themes and none about peace. Clearly war is the better seller.

This is not at all surprising when we consider how our nation and its people of all races and creeds have been scarred by war over the years and this touches close to home. My granddaughter, Maev Rose, graduated from high school in 2016 and joined the U.S. Marine Corps. She sees how evil continues to crawl across the face of our planet, even here in the United States, and wanted to do something about it. Before she left for Boot Camp, we had a chance to sit down together and talk about our family traditions. I told her she was our sixth generation warrior and the first woman.

Her uncle, Ted, served in Desert Storm in the early 1990s when his Army Reserve outfit was activated. I was a Vietnam Era veteran in the U.S. Army on active duty, active reserve, and later intelligence from 1959 to 1968. Her great grandfather, Stan Sr., was in World War II. His Army Unit was scheduled to be a part of the D-Day Invasion of Normandy. He contracted pneumonia and was in bed on a hospital ship when the first salvo of nearby battleship cannon fire devastated the French coastline. He said the concussion was so strong it knocked him onto the floor. My grandfather on my mother's side, Sanford G. Ware, was in a supply unit in France in World War I and my great-grandfather on my father's side was a Sergeant-Major in the Scots Guard in England and fought in the first Boer War in South Africa in the early 1880s. Each served honorably and willingly and that calling has touched the soul of our newest generation.

With so many generations impacted by war is there any hope for peace? And what is the definition of "peace" anyway?

Webster's Collegiate Dictionary defines peace as: "*1. A pact or agreement to end hostilities. 2. A state of tranquility or quiet, esp.: a. freedom from civil disturbance or war. b. public order or security, as provided by law. 3. Harmony in personal relations, mutual concord.4. Freedom from fear, agitating passions, moral conflict.*"

With these parameters in mind, we can now walk through the pages of this publication with a shared point of reference. The critical question continues to rise up, is there any hope for peace in our time, in our communities, and in our hearts? I haven't given up yet. Maybe there is something to the old saying, "hope springs eternal". May my writing efforts bring a sense of hope to each and every one of us.

AN AMERICAN INDIAN CREATION STORY

Creator-God stood on the Mount and looked at all He'd made.
North, South, East, and West, He liked what He surveyed.

Mother Earth sat by His side, a tear was in her eye.
Creator-God looked with concern, "Tell me why you cry."
"I'm lonely."
"How could this be? I am always with you."
"You made me to be a Mother, but I have no children."

Creator-God took some clay and formed a Mortal Man.
With infinite variety, He continued with His plan.
Two-legs, four-legs, flyers, and those who swim.
All felt the warming sun and a sacred breath from Him.

Mother-Earth spread her arms and pulled them to her breast.
"I love you all, my children, from the great to very least."
Ha-Gue-A-Dees-Sas

WE HAVE ONLY ONE PLANET

People! People! ...Listen up!
The estimated population of the United States of America exceeds 323,000,000 men, women and children. Where do all these people live and what is happening to our environment?

I found my grandfather's 1944 State Farm Road Atlas, published by Rand McNally and Company. I wondered how the populations of random American cities had changed over the years. Here are some examples:

City	1944	2016	City	1944	2016
Boston, MA	770,826	673,184	Philadelphia, PA	1,931,334	1,568,000
Atlanta, GA	302,288	472,522	Miami, FL	172,172	453,579
Houston, TX	384,514	2,303,000	Phoenix, AZ	63,414	1,615,000
St. Louis, MO	816,048	315,685	Denver, CO	322,412	682,545
Las Vegas, NV	8422	632,912	Los Angeles, CA	1,504,277	3,976,000
Seattle, WA	368,302	704,352	Minneapolis, MN	492,370	413,651
Chicago, IL	3,396,808	2,705,000	Detroit, MI	1,623,452	672,795
Slippery Rock, PA (I just like the name of that town)				1269	3583

Clearly, over the past eighty years or so there has been a population shift southward and westward. In fact, of the twenty-five largest cities in the United States, seventeen are in the geographic areas mentioned.

The population of the country as a whole is growing by over two million people per year. Over half are new births and the remainder is from legal and illegal immigration. The Global Footwork Network Data warns that our nation can self-sustain a population of only about one hundred and fifty million if we work to reduce consumption levels.

Many reliable sources mention that the planet Earth could not survive another United States. Let's look over some facts to support that premise.

In terms of damage to the planet, they argue that three hundred and twenty three million Americans create a greater environmental impact than one and a half billion Chinese or over one billion people from India. Our country has less than five percent of the world's population but uses twenty-five percent of all oil, twenty-three percent of all coal products, and twenty-seven percent of all the aluminum manufactured.

The Natural Resources Council estimates that Americans consume one-third of all paper and generate nearly three-quarters of the world's toxic waste. Almost one-third of the world's automobiles drive as many miles in our country as the rest of the world combined and are the primary producers of greenhouse gases. One out of every five Americans is dependent on water contaminated by lead, over-chlorination, toxic chemicals, or fecal bacteria. As a result 42.6 billion one-liter bottles of water were inventoried and sold in 2015. The resulting decline in surface water levels from coast to coast has coincided with a nation-wide increase in water pollution. The latest estimates say that forty percent of our rivers, forty-six percent of our lakes, and fifty percent of all estuaries are too polluted for fishing or safe swimming.

We have lost ninety percent of our old growth forests due to logging, population expansion, and forest fires and only about one percent of native prairies still exist. Because of urban and suburban sprawl, an area the size of Delaware is paved over every year. Because of the air pollution produced by our excesses, sixty thousand of our brothers and sisters die prematurely each year from cardiopulmonary conditions.

This paints a mind-boggling picture of our nation and its people. It appears we are so wrapped up in our own selfishness and excesses that we are impervious to the damage being caused. Clearly, it is time for each of us to think about our actions and try to determine how to be better. Really it is very, very simple. Let this be our mantra:

"Live simply, so people can simply live"

* * * * * * * * * *

Stormy Weather

Harvey, Irma, Jose, Lee, Nate, Maria, Florence and Michael? No, what happened during the autumn of 2017 and 2018 was not the name of the kids in a high school glee club. In less than five weeks in 2017 six major hurricanes roared out of the eastern Atlantic Ocean and, without any sense of conscience, destroyed everything in their paths. Harvey devastated the Houston, Texas area on August 25th and by the time it had moved on it had killed eighty-two people and caused an estimated $180 billion in destruction. Sustained winds of 130 mph damaged 135,000 homes displaced thirteen million people and dumped as much as fifty inches of rain on parts of the city. Jose thundered at 150 mph into the eastern Caribbean leaving Barbuda and some smaller islands in shambles before moving eastward out to sea again. With Irma right behind, it was the first time and so far the only time in Atlantic recorded history that two active hurricanes simultaneously had recorded speeds of at least 150 mph. Irma roared across the eastern Caribbean islands killing thirty-eight with 175 mph winds. While still at sea, the winds were clocked at 185 mph, the highest ever recorded. When it reached Florida on September 10th it was a Category 4 storm that killed an additional thirty-four people and took out power to 6.8 million users. The total devastation has been estimated

3

as easily $100 billion with Cuba and some of the smaller islands suffering even more losses. Maria attacked another group of Caribbean Islands then smashed into Puerto Rico on September 20th with 155 mph winds. The entire island was without electric power, thousands of people lost their lives and homes, and agriculture were destroyed. Combined with heavy flooding, this was the worst storm to ravage the island in over eighty years. Just as people were trying to recover from the devastation, Nate came on the scene, killed twenty-two people in Central America, and then hit New Orleans dead on as a Category 1 storm. The country had just begun to recover when in 2018 Florence and Michael showed up causing a combined 34 billion dollars in damage.

What is this "Category" description? American weather systems use the Saffir-Simpson Hurricane Wind Scale to explain the intensity of the storms. Here is that scale:

Category One ... Sustained wind speeds of 74 to 95 mph.
Category Two ... Sustained wind speeds of 96 to 110 mph.
Category Three ...Sustained wind speeds of 111 to 129 mph.
Category Four... Sustained wind speeds of 130 to 156 mph
Category Five ... Sustained wind speeds of 157 mph or higher

Experts said that 2017, with warmer than normal sea temperatures and winds that eventually turn into hurricanes as they sweep across the ocean, appears to be the most active year for major storms on record. The Atlantic hurricane season runs from June 1 to November 30 with the peak occurring between mid-August and late October. Threats from hurricanes include high winds, heavy rainfall, storm surge, coastal and inland flooding, rip currents, and even tornadoes. Looking back over the past thirty years, no one has seen so many major hurricanes with such devastating repercussions on life and property. The federal government has kept yearly weather information for almost 170 years, which provides data for comparison. In fact, the 2020 hurricane season was so active that forecasters ran out of names for the storms.

Does this imply that global warming is looming on the horizon and is somehow responsible for the problems? Scientists caution it is too soon to draw conclusions from the data and they don't necessarily confirm that a trend is forming that we need to worry about. Comparing year-by-year information is difficult because often through the years storms that developed then abated while still at sea, despite their intensity, may have gone unnoticed. Contemporary communication and news service has never been better so even though serious weather situations may have swept across the eastern rim of the Western Hemisphere in past years, it is not inconceivable that most people didn't know about it. With satellites and airplane monitoring, weather forecasters are now more attuned to what is developing as far away as the west coast of Africa and can endeavor to predict possible problems well before they reach our doorstep. Also, the category scale was not in use until the late 1960's.

So, how can we prepare for future hurricanes as indications say things could very well get worse?

Know your local hurricane evacuation routes and have a plan for where you can stay once you are out of the dangerous conditions. Find out if your community has some kind of text or e-mail alerting system and sign up.

Put together a go-bag disaster supply kit including a flashlight and batteries, cash, first aid supplies, medications, and copies of your critical information if you need to evacuate.

If you choose to ride out a hurricane, plan for adequate supplies in case you lose power and water for several days. Even though later you might change your mind, you might not be able to leave due to flooding or blocked roads.

The government suggests you make a family emergency communication plan and has an outline at: http://www.ready.gov/make-a-plan.

How can I prepare my home for the upcoming storm?

Winds take a serious toll on trees and foliage. Trim and remove dangerous trees and limbs that may hit the house.

Secure loose rain gutters and downspouts and clear away any clogged areas of debris to prevent water damage.

Reduce property damage by retrofitting to secure and reinforce the roof, windows, and doors, including the garage door.

Purchase a portable power generator for use during power outages. Remember to keep generators and other alternate power and heat sources outside and at least twenty feet away from windows and doors. Never plug a generator into a wall outlet.

Consider building a "safe room" in the house to protect from high winds and flooding. The government has some suggestions at: http://www.fema.gov/safe-rooms.

We must believe that more intense storms are what scientists expect to see as the planet's climate changes because of warmer ocean water and a comparatively high salinity rate which are fuel for hurricanes. People who are following the hurricane issue say to expect rising seas, stronger winds, and almost immeasurable rainfall amounts. It is important to better understand this current intense period to save lives and prevent worse future destruction.

* * * * * * * * * *

Conflict in 'Indian Country'

Two American Indian professional people were driving along a highway that separated an Indian reservation from private land. The landowner had developed his property into a prosperous sprinkler-irrigated vegetable farm. Although each year's crop was a little less bountiful, he was making a fine living. The land on the other side of the road was left in its natural state. Sagebrush and tufts of grass fought with the sandy soil, constant wind, and meager water supply for life and had done so since the beginning.

The driver shook his head at the difference between the two sides of the highway. "What a waste," he commented.

The passenger nodded in agreement.

What neither realized until they discussed this incident later in the day was that the comment "what a waste" was applied in two diametrically opposed points of view. The driver saw the private land being dressed, tilled, and kept until it resembled an American Garden of Eden. The Indian land was being left idle and its potential worth was wasted year after year. The passenger knew that the crops being grown were not indigenous to the area and were continually draining the soil of its nutrients while the irrigation slowly leeched salts into the earth until someday it would be barren and lifeless for eternity. The Indian land was the way it always had been and would be that way for generations to come. He felt a sense of comfort knowing his children and their children would always be able to enjoy the land as their ancestors had.

This incident illustrates an important situation facing Native people that they have wrestled with for many years. What to do with the natural resources found on the land set aside for them as reservations. When the Federal Government decided where to establish the reservations, they had scouts and military engineers determine the most supposedly useless land that the Manifest Destiny believers would not be interested in. Ironically, in some cases this land has proven to be quite valuable. Marketable mineral resources have been found in many locations, as well as oil and natural gas. Fishing and hunting opportunities attract outdoorsmen who are willing to pay licensing fees and accommodation charges to take advantage of what is being offered. Forests, natural pharmaceuticals, and grasslands grace the land and can be profitable and provide much needed revenue to the tribes and bands.

Another issue making itself known has appeared on the horizon, water. The cities of North America are blossoming from coast to coast and are thirstily using fresh water in vast amounts. In the less-populated areas, more and more farm people are finding ways to bring irrigation to formerly dry land farming areas. In all cases the amount of fresh water is a finite resource whether pumped out of the ground or brought to the waiting users by canal, aqueduct, or pipeline. Consider this, great amounts of usable surface water have their sources on Indian land. As the Western Hemisphere walks into the twenty-first century, this may become one of the most important issues for survival of the Euro-American culture, unless they finally get serious about desalination projects. Native people could very well be in the position of making some important decisions about who gets the water and how much it will cost them. Although not the only location in our country, the Southwestern area of the United States has an exceptionally growing need for clean water as the population expands. A person needs to only fly over the Phoenix, Arizona, or the Los Angeles, California basin to get a feel for the vast numbers of people living there.

Indian reservations are legally considered as "sovereign nations" and the courts have repeatedly honored this concept. They have the decision-making ability considering their natural resources. Possibility: A large Indian reservation in northeastern Washington state is bounded on the east and south by the 150-mile long Lake Franklin D. Roosevelt. It is the largest lake in the state with 125 square miles of surface area and a depth of up to 375 feet. It is less than forty miles from the northern boundary of the reservation to the Canadian border. Consider the effects downriver if the Natives negotiated a deal to build a pipeline to carry water to thirsty Canadians and pumped it out of the lake. Far-fetched? Maybe not. When the monumental Grand Coulee Dam in Washington State was constructed in the

1930s, the Columbia Basin Reclamation Project emerged. There was a need to provide a water source to irrigate the sandy desert soil southward from the river. The U.S. government constructed two rock-faced, earth-filled dams over 120 feet high, one across the northern end of a nearby coulee (canyon) and another across the southern end some twenty-seven miles away. Then they pumped water out of the river, filled the coulee, and made Banks Lake to a depth of 117 feet which provides a constant source for the Main Canal which irrigates 670,000 acres of farmland.

What about the land itself? Historically, American Indians have always believed that the land was not only perfect, it was sacred. It provides all that is needed and does not belong to anybody. The ethics of land ownership came with the incursion of the European conquest of North America and today is so deep into contemporary society that it has become a normal part of thought and deed for us all, including reservation occupants.

A quandary emerges when a tribe or band decides to change the land by constructing large structures like gambling casinos, parking garages, hotels, or bingo parlors. The land is cleared and leveled then the structures are cut into the earth, concreted, walled, and roofed to last for a hundred years. Often they are larger than warehouses or school buildings and are built to hold hundreds of customers. As a result the "sacred" land is skimmed to the very earth itself and a roadway and huge parking lot is paved and covers the landscape forever. Sewage systems bore through the terrain seeking outlets for the fecal effluent being carried away from the buildings. Sometimes it ends up in ground water that has been interrupted by diking, fill-dirt, and gravel. The problem compounds itself because the very same land that is good for constructing buildings and parking lots is also necessary for survival and sustenance. People who follow these trends say we are losing over three million acres of arable land a year to population growth and businesses.

The land in its natural state was always considered an integral part of the sacred circle of life to traditionalists. It saddens concerned people to realize that the circle is being broken, this time by Indians themselves. It was often the elders who spoke out against the plans when extensive building projects were begun on Indian land. They knew how serious these decisions can be and that the ramifications would be long-lasting. These learned people lived with the "seven generations decision process" which caused leaders to look well into the future to try to prophesy how an idea might affect their children, their children's children, and so forth. This was contrasted against the immediate value of a project when it comes to providing jobs and increasing revenue. As the tribes and bands continue to be pressured to use their land for non-traditional purposes, there will always be constant turmoil between what has been and what will be. This contradiction in their lifestyles exacts its toll on their spirits and their basic essence. A break in the sacred circle affects everyone young and old.

* * * * * * * * * *

Every Part of the Earth is Sacred to my People
In 1854, Chief Seattle, leader of the Suquamish Tribe, gave a speech to mark the transfer of ancestral Indian lands to the United States government. Here is part of that speech:

"The Great Chief in Washington sends word that he wishes to buy our land. The Great Chief also sends us words of friendship and good will. This is kind of him, since we know he has little need for our friendship in return. But we will consider your offer. For we know that if we do not sell, the white man may come with guns and take our land.

"How can you buy or sell the sky, the warmth of the land? The idea is strange to us. If we do not own the freshness of the air and the sparkle of the water, how can you buy them?

Every part of this earth is sacred to my people. Every shining pine needle, every sandy shore, every mist in the dark woods, every clearing and humming insect is holy in the memory and experience of my people. The sap which courses through the trees carries the memories of the red man.

"The white man's dead forgot the country of their birth when they go to walk among the stars. Our dead never forget this beautiful earth, for it is the mother of the red man. We are part of the earth and it is part of us. The perfumed flowers are our sisters; the deer, the horse, the great eagle, these are our brothers.

"We will consider your offer to buy our land. But is will not be easy. For this land is sacred to us.

"If we decide to accept your offer, I will make one condition: the white man must treat the beasts of this land as his brothers. Whatever happens to the beasts, soon happens to man. All things are connected. Teach your children what we have taught our children that the earth is our mother. Whatever befalls the earth befalls the children of the earth.

"One thing we know which the white man may soon discover, our God is the same God. This earth is precious to Him, and to harm the earth is to heap contempt on its Creator. Even the white man cannot be exempt from the common destiny. We may be brothers after all. We shall see."

Our Hope for Peace – Our Children

I have studied children in the school setting from 1963 to 2003 as a janitor, student teacher, teacher, administrator, and college supervisor. I have seen them at their very best and, unfortunately, at their very worse.

The public elementary school is in many ways a microcosm of what might be best described as "the real world." Interpersonal relationships are practiced and fine-tuned. Potential leaders find special skills, develop them, and begin to emerge. Follower-types acquiesce and eventually blend into the crowd. Life-long friendships are established and are fondly recalled long after the actual school days have wandered into the mist of fading memories. Equally as important, children acquire knowledge and socialization as much by observation and exploration as by study and recitation. Children somehow learn how to deal with success and how to cope with adversity. What they will become as adults begins to manifest itself within their small bodies. It is an exciting and as well as a frightening journey for them.

Consider some of the following glimpses into their marvelous world ...

* * * * * * * * *

The Pledge of Allegiance

I remember so clearly some years ago when he came to our school. This young Vietnamese boy had survived the horrors of the Southeast Asian war but still carried the scars on his soul as well as his body. Old beyond his ten or eleven years, his eyes mirrored distrust and fearfulness. A religious group had brought his family and him to the United States, but despite the safety of his new homeland, he felt displaced and alienated from those around him. He seemed most comfortable around the adults of our elementary school and we accepted him warmly. His father and older brothers had been conscripted into combat never to be seen again, so his mother and older sisters served as the nurturers in his life. He was our special "Boat Person" and emerged as one of the most precious flowers in our school garden. We enrolled him in our English as a Second Language program and endeavored to mainstream him into regular classes as his proficiency improved.

Now it was time for our spring-time Awards Ceremony and I asked him if he would be willing to lead our school in the Pledge of Allegiance. He did a beautiful job. Each word was pronounced perfectly and with honest feeling. Even the children who had droned these words toward the wall their entire school careers knew this was something special.

"… one nation, under God, indivisible with liberty and justice for all … Amen."

Smiles turned to quiet chuckles as six hundred children and a large group of staff and parents began to realize the unusual ending.

He just shrugged his shoulders and said in the microphone, "Well, it seems like a prayer to me …"

I thought about his words and began to wonder if the other children really knew how significant the Pledge of Allegiance actually was. In my opinion it has always been one of the most important promises ever made and should not be taken lightly. I decided to drop by some of the classrooms during opening to find out for myself how the Pledge was perceived by the reciters and alerted the staff to my plan. After a few visits it appeared that the Pledge was one of the demands of a very busy school day and had to be dealt with as painlessly and as quickly as possible.

The little kindergartners stood tall and proud. Most had their right hands over their hearts. One young student was moving his hand across his chest with a look of dismay on his face. Apparently, he was having trouble locating his heart.

The teacher tried to dispel his discomfort by saying kindly, "Just rest your hand on your shirt for a second. When your hand is over your heart you will be able to feel it beating."

As the other classmates waited patiently, he made a few tries then blurted out in frustration, "But my heart doesn't stick out as much as yours does."

I could feel the laughter begin to well up inside me as the teacher turned and looked at me with what could best be described as shock. After a few deep breaths, she regained her composure and continued the Pledge exercise.

They began to chant, "I plee-za wee-jance."

We had our work cut out for us. Each classroom teacher was asked to take some time to be sure the children understood the words to the Pledge of Allegiance accurately and to explain what it was all about. I offered to come by and talk to the classrooms if needed and I would be visiting individual students in the near future as a progress check.

Ronnie was wearing his new Tiger Cub Scout bandana and navy blue shirt. He would serve as my first interviewee. "It means you put your two fingers in one eye and don't let it touch the ground." He was learning the Cub Scout salute as well as flag protocol. Apparently he had mixed the messages somewhat

Aedyn and Tristan were side-by-side at their work table. They stood by their chairs and placed their hands over their hearts as they accurately recited the Pledge. They explained to me, "It means like the Army and remembering all the people who died in the war."

Despite the singularity of their response, I felt they were beginning to get the point and were just about ready for some exposure to concepts like "freedom" and "liberty."

Amanda said the words clearly and with confidence. When I asked if she knew what was said, she responded, "My friend's mom and dad had a big fight so she is staying with us for a while."

Apparently, she had other things on her mind and wanted to share them with her principal. Sometimes the trials of everyday living supersede the intellectualizing of some of our most sacred rites and rituals.

It was now approaching Memorial Day. Our all-school assembly had been labored over, massaged and fine-tuned, and was ready to roll. The United States Air Force Reserve honor band was going to perform as part of the festivities. The children were totally transfixed when they walked onto the stage in their impressive uniforms and shiny instruments. Hadley, our student body president, led the assembly in the Pledge of Allegiance then turned the microphone over to me for introductions. As he stepped away from the rostrum to return to his seat, I called him back. "Do you know what we all just did?" I inquired.

He looked at me somewhat confused and responded, "The Pledge of Allegiance."

"But do you understand what we just did?" I continued.

We sat down side-by-side on the steps in front of the stage as the entire student body, staff and parents watched in silence. The teachers had no idea what I was about to unfold and I noted their nervousness. Was I testing them publicly to see if they had clarified the Pledge to their students?

Stanza by stanza, I recited the Pledge in the microphone and asked Hadley to extemporaneously explain in his own words what they meant:

"I pledge allegiance… what does that mean?"

"I promise to be on your side."

"…and to the republic for which it stands."

"I don't know… America?"

As we continued, I could see the discomfort building up in this young person. He was on the spot in front of the entire school community and our honored guests. I was sorry for putting him through this, but I felt it was extremely important.

In frustration, his face began to get flushed and he blurted out, "I don't know! You make us do it!"

I continued, trying to ignore his reaction. After each verse he really did beautifully.

"With liberty and justice for all." Then I paused and asked him, "Does that mean kids, too?"

He looked at me with a confused expression, thought for a moment, and then replied firmly, "Yes it does! Just because we are kids doesn't mean we don't have any rights!"

The entire audience burst out in spontaneous applause, kids, adults, and even the band members. In a few brief moments, at the beginning of an elementary school Memorial Day program, I felt a group of people matured a little as Americans on that special day.

Even the music seemed more beautiful.

* * * * * * *

Hallways and Swing Sets
It is what it is…

Some of the children I had the most trouble with turned out to be the ones I liked the most, despite themselves. Too many young people wander through the public school system with a bundle of baggage on their backs that would break down an ox. We endeavor to establish an environment that is supportive and reasonably safe for six or seven hours a day but it is only a small part of each child's existence. Their homes and neighborhoods are their 'real world' and we are pretty much helpless to make things better.

Tanisha was a large and imposing sixth grader. She had decided she was the boss of the playground and it didn't take long for her to communicate that fact to the rest of the children. The adult recess supervisors did not buy that for a minute, so there was bound to be a collision of conviction and what always results is that the principal is called into the fray.

I professed what was called an Assertive Discipline program. It included pre-communicated incremental responses to specific infractions and also positive reinforcement for correct behavior. The breakdown is when a student refuses to buy into the process or when the parent component becomes ineffective, either because of the school's inability to connect with the parent or the parent's refusal or inability to follow-up.

In Tanisha's situation, it became clear early that we were pretty much on our own. The school district has Behavior Intervention classrooms for the students who continue to disrupt the educational process, but these are often the last chances before the children are removed permanently from the school system and find themselves under State mandated supervision and/or on the streets. In no way did I want to basically "throw away" Tanisha, but I was running out of options.

As she sat in my office with an annoying petulant expression on her face, I blurted out, "Why are you in so much trouble?"

She seemed surprised by my question, thought for a moment then responded, "I've always been in trouble. I don't remember when I wasn't on somebody's shit list. That's who I am. I've got to be me."

In frustration all I could do was say, "In-school suspension. Go get your school work and report to the 'cubbie' outside my office."

I had set up a cubical where a student was removed from the flow of the school day and where I could more or less keep an eye on him or her.

Later, I sat down with her teacher, Mr. Fuller, and we discussed some strategies. Despite her behavior and attitude she was very bright and had terrific potential if we could somehow round off the rough edges. He agreed to pretty much take her under his wing and provide extra positive attention and some one-on-one counseling. One of the issues he talked to her about was her bad language on the playground, since this was often predictive behavior that led to more serious and too often physical confrontations. It was pretty obvious she was modeling language she heard in the home and had a hard time understanding why that talk in the school setting was very inappropriate. That afternoon the teacher stopped by my office, sat down in a chair, and shook his head.

"How did things go with Tanisha today?" I inquired. I had a pretty good idea what his response was about to shared.

"We got to talking about her bad language on the school grounds and how it gets her into trouble and leads into more serious situations.

I tried to be careful letting her know that how people talk at home is for home, but it not okay at school. She seemed to really take it to heart and I could see her processing what I was saying and what the consequences usually were. She looked up at me and said 'God damn it, Mr. Fuller, you ain't throwin' crap. You are right on!'"

I want to be an Indian

Little Emily was six years old, came home from school, and told her mom she wanted to look like an Indian. Her mom wondered how she could make this happen and began to sketch out a plan. She decided she could sew a cloth vest with frills and felt marker Indian designs. Maybe make a headband out of decorative elastic and a fake bow and arrow from a tree branch and some twine. A little make-up for war paint and that would complete the project.

When she shared her ideas with Emily, her child looked at her like she had lost her mind. She wanted her mom to sew a colorful sari.

Welcome to the Family

I was standing in the hallway after school as two little second-graders hurried by clearly in some degree of stress. They were on their way to a Bluebirds meeting in the library. The child leading the charge was one of our little blonde-haired, blue-eyed angels. The child running behind was one of our black students and I heard her say, "What if they won't let me in the meeting?"

The little person in front replied, "If they won't let you in, I'll tell them you are my sister."

Comeuppance

They sat huddled together, tearful and painfully anxious, trying to find some solace in the nearness of each other. Three third grade girls in deep trouble, looking like small colorful birds in their brightly colored coats, snow pants, and boots, waiting quietly in the outer office to see the principal.

A potentially serious incident had occurred on the playground during morning recess. One of the playground supervisors and the school's custodian had carried the world's meanest fourth-grader into the health room across the hall from the secretary's office. He had been partially buried in a snow bank, as much in shock as in pain. Now, he lay moaning on a cot, ice-encrusted and hurt or possibly wounded. The school nurse was trying to determine the extent of his injuries and the appropriate response as he tearfully implicated the perpetrators who had caused this grievous act. Although it did not appear to be a "call 9-1-1" situation, the universal cure-all for all playground injuries, an ice pack, would have definitely added insult to injury.

Now it was time for another case of my Solomon-like adjudication.

In my most professional principal's voice and with a stern no-nonsense look, I called the girls into the office, considered an inner-sanctum of mystery and fear. Rumor has it that some children went into the office never to return. These three little birds were especially fearful because they had never been in trouble in school before.

I sat them down and then stood over them demanding, "I want the whole story. The entire truth."

After a prolonged silence, Robin asserted herself as the spokesperson, "It's all his fault, Mr. Hughes."

"His fault?" I replied incredulously, "As best I can tell he is the one who has been hurt. Maybe seriously."

Robin continued, "He waits around until we make a nice snow fort. Just about the time we are ready to play in it, he runs at us as fast as he can and crashes it down."

The other two nodded in earnest agreement.

Unimpressed, I said, "So-o-o?"

"That's not fair! We're tired of it!"

"So-o-o?"

They looked at each other, then Melody's small voice continues the explanation, "This time we built our snow fort over one of the bike racks."

Trying to maintain my composure as best I could, I ordered them, "Don't move a muscle. Any of you. I'll be right back!" I made a bee-line for the staff lavatory, so I could laugh myself breathless. The mental image of the world's meanest fourth-grader doing a 360-degree flip in the air repeated itself over and over.

I think it's called "natural consequences."

The Foulest Foul

Both fifth-graders were soiled and disheveled as they were brought into my office, but then most fifth-graders look that way by the end of a school day. It was difficult to tell who the winner was and who the loser. The discipline referral slip stated simply, "Fighting".

The look on Heather's tear-streaked face was one of righteous indignation and total anger. It was clear that no matter what was about to happen, her previous transgression was worth the price about to be paid. The boy was crouching in the chair next to her. His body language telling me he wished he was someplace else, anyplace else.

I set the stage with the obvious, "You two have been at this school a long time. You know we do not tolerate fighting of any kind" Someday a student is going to say to me that if I know he knows it, why am I telling him? "Fighting is not acceptable and never necessary."

"It was this time," mumbled the young lady.

I had a pretty good idea a difficult situation was developing before me. "Why do you say that?" I responded.

"He tripped me!" she stated flatly.

The boy glared at her and exclaimed, "Did not! You fell over you own big feet!"

"Did not! You tripped me with your own big fat foot!" The derision was clear in her voice.

"Did not! I was going for the ball!"

The debate continued before me as if I were not there. The outcome of a playground touch football game was the center of each child's life at that moment. The young girl, fleet of foot and athletic, had caught a thrown ball, broke away from the crowd, and was heading for "daylight". The boy could not quite catch up with her, so he tripped her. She reacted by getting up and punching him in the mouth and the melee ensued.

I could feel the frustration in both children. The young lady was one step from victory before it was snatched away. The boy was outdone by a girl!

I realized how important the "sorting out" of children was during their elementary school years. The boy was not going to let the girl climb up one rung higher on the ladder of success without a battle. I wondered why he felt diminished in the face of her elevation. Does this phenomenon continue to manifest itself even into our adult years?

Few elementary school playground "superstars" emerge as excellent athletes in later years. There may be a sense of how fleeting dominance is during the pre-adolescent years and an inner feeling of frustration in the early developers as the late-bloomers begin to catch up. After her senior year in high school, the young lady earned a full-ride scholarship to play college level women's basketball. The boy walked off into life and I never heard about him again.

To this day, I send him a special wish that he is okay and hope he has found his own form of success.

"Who Ordered the Poo-poo Platter?"

We called it the "multi-purpose room". It served as the gym for physical education classes and was turned into the lunchroom during the mid-day break. Every major school event from student performances to the annual P.T.A. carnival was held there. In the spring time as the weather warms, the outside doors were propped open in an effort to cool down the location.

A young first-grader was sitting at his lunch table quietly crying. The lunch supervisor approached him to find out what was wrong. All he could do was shake his head. Concerned that something very serious must be happening in his life, she called me from the school office for assistance. I sat down by him and asked if I could help in any way.

He looked at me with watery eyes and choked, "A bird pooped on my lunch."

I paused a moment not expecting any response even remotely like that, then clarified, "Now, that can't happen. We are inside. All the birds are outside in the trees around the playground."

He pointed at the white splatter on his macaroni and cheese, then pointed at the ceiling. Sure enough, sitting in the rafters was a young starling carpet-bombing the table under him.

Eventually, the perpetrator flew out the open door leaving an extra bit of work for our day custodian. The hungry young man and I went over to the head cook to explain what had happened. She laughed so hard her face turned beet red, then she found him a replacement lunch plus a Fudgesicle for his troubles.

Snowsuit Confusion

Winter time in the American Snow Belt brings extra responsibilities for the primary level school teachers. An especially trying one is helping the children put on or take off their snow gear.

A particular kindergartener was having some difficulty donning his boots and snowsuit in preparation for the end of his school day. It was becoming clear that the snowsuit was probably from last winter and was no longer the correct size, which added to the efforts needed. The teacher began helping the child and their combined efforts successfully paid off. With continued determination, the zipper was closed and he was ready to go.

He looked up and down at his clothing and said, "It's not my snow-suit."

The teacher rolled her eyes and began the unpleasant task of un-doing all their hard work. As she pulled the legs of the snowsuit past his feet he said, "It's my brother's."

Keep Your Eyes on the Prize

While engaged in a classroom observation, the school secretary called me on the wall phone to please report to the office. There was an emergency.

As I hurried down the hallway, I saw her quickly coming my way, visually distressed. When we met, without speaking she opened her hand and displayed a glass eye, pupil out. One of our primary grade students needed the eye and it apparently had fallen out. Understand-ably, the teacher sent the child to the office.

Even today, I still cannot explain why, but because of the ludicrous-ness of the situation I started laughing so hard I had to lean against the wall. The secretary saw absolutely no humor in at at all!

I was going to ask her if she had tried to re-insert it herself, but clearly this was an inappropriate response and I kept my mouth shut.

We returned to the health room and I visited with the student while the secretary called her mother for instructions concerning how to cor-rectly return the jewel to its proper location.

Pine Cones – Oh My!

She was a fourth-grader. Small in stature with close-cropped blonde hair. She could have modeled for Little Debbie snack cakes. but she was the terror of the playground. In a few brief months she had rumbled through the school's discipline plan like a tank. I had called her mother so many times people were beginning to think we had a thing going.

I didn't want to keep her in time-out the rest of her life and I certainly didn't want to suspend or expel her in the fourth grade! She needed to be out in the fresh air, running off her ample supply of energy and her two-liter bottle of carbonation. So I tried something different.

"Cholie, if you ever want to have another recess at this school, I want you to pick up all the pine cones along the north fence of the playground. Get a plastic garbage can and some gloves from Gary the Custodian and go to work. When the playground is spotless, I'll inspect it and if it passes, we will try letting you have your recesses back."

The custodian and I watched her from the school's back door and she seemed pretty serious about getting the job done. After a couple days she asked to see me in a very complacent manner.

"Mr. Hughes, I pick up pine cones and the next day I go out and there are just as many on the ground as I had picked up. I'll never get the playground clean."

At last, I had finally made an impression. "I'll make you a deal. I'm going to give you back your recesses. If you can stay out of trouble, you'll never have to pick up any more pine cones."

I didn't see her for discipline problems the rest of the years she attended our elementary school.

A Gentle Hand and a Nurturing Nature

With hundreds of children in proximity of each other, sooner or later accidents do occur. A primary-aged child fell out of a swing backwards and hit the pea gravel with a shrill scream of fear and pain. Tim, a quiet fourth-grader that was seldom noticed, pushed his way through the gathering crowd of onlookers. "Be careful! Don't move her! Somebody get the duty person! You and you!"

Moments later the playground supervisors arrived on the scene to see Tim talking to the injured student and endeavoring to comfort her. Thankfully, the child just had the wind knocked out of her and soon was ambulatory and being taken to the school office health room for closer inspection. The supervisory aide recorded the incident then peeked into my office to let me know what had happened. She felt that some special recognition was due for Tim.

I called him to my office, welcomed him warmly and inquired, "How did you know what to do?"

"I dunno. I just thought about what I would want to happen if it was me on the ground," he responded.

I looked closely at this young African-American boy. His teacher Mrs. Betts had shared with me earlier in the school year some of her concerns. Tim never seemed to try very hard to "fit in". He worked hard but never asserted himself academically or socially. She had to take special effort to get his classmates to include him in the ongoing educational and social flow of the classroom.

He was a child with those too rare and special qualities of empathy and gentleness. I could not help but spread my wings out to uplift this unique individual. While he was in our school I tried to find ways to connect him with as many other students as possible and he was willing to participate in school crossing guard, committee work, cross-age student tutoring, student council, and after-school activities. Tim touched a number of children's lives during those fleeting moments he was with us. We all saw this fine young man in light of the content of his character and in light of his efforts.

Some years later, I sadly read in the local newspaper that a young teenager about the age he would have been and with a similar name was killed in a drive-by shooting one rainy Northwest night. The authorities called it "gang-related" and had no definite leads at that time. As I felt the sadness well-up inside I despaired for a wasted life. Whether or not it was actually was "our Tim", it still was a tragedy.

* * * * * * * * * *

HUGHES

Our Hope for Peace – Finding Our 'Quiet Place'

Across all of the major religions, prophets and scribes realized the importance of seeking out quiet and isolated places where they could recharge their batteries, meditate, pray to God, and hear the messages needing to be taken to the faithful. Whether it was forty days and forty nights in the desert or sojourns to a Cave on Mt. Hira, the importance of getting away was paramount. We will never fully realize how exhausting these responsibilities were to the important pillars of our faiths, so these sacred locations were also where they could retreat from the demands of their followers and find needed energy knowing they would have to continue the good fight.

The Indigenous People of America seemed to know where to go to communicate with the Creator. "Power Centers" were revealed to them in ancient times and this information was handed down generation to generation. They were utilized with appropriate respect and ceremony and an important part of their culture. Many of these "high places" were focused in the vicinity of significant geographical features. The Four Corners area of the Navaho Reservation, Mt. Shasta in northern California, Mt. Rainier and Mt. St. Helens in Washington State, the Medicine Wheel in the Big Horn Mountains and also Devils Tower in Wyoming, Bear Butte in western South Dakota, Niagara Falls and the Herkimer area of New York, Mt. Washington in New

Hampshire, the Great Smokey Mountains of Virginia and Tennessee, Mammoth Cave in Kentucky, and the Burial Mounds area of southern Illinois just to name a few.

Within these special areas, the Natives sought out caves, waterfalls, secluded forested and meadow areas, plateaus, isolated rock formations, high mountain lakes, and special river bank areas to perform the appropriate rites and rituals for meditation and prayer. Often, they were marked with some special sign to help the petitioner to find the exact location. This might have been a rune carved on an entrance rock or a tree trunk or a marker like a totem pole or decorated coupe stick. The lamentations of the issue continue even unto today as we realize that when the white man arrived on the scene not only did he mindlessly desecrate these time-honored places, but he might have carelessly destroyed the markers so even if someone was seeking that special power center it was impossible to find anymore.

An interesting side-bar to this situation came to my attention recently. A Native Shaman showed me a map of North America that featured power centers on the continent. Many, many of them contained the largest cities of our nation. It appears that innately, the new Americans knew where to settle down and build their homes and futures. Was it some sort of message sent by generations of Native worshippers that "this is the place" or did it have more to do with geography?

* * * * * * * * * *

The reality of today's world is that despite our need to pray and meditate, it is pretty much impossible to be able to drop everything and take off into the forest or to descend into an isolated grotto for a number of days of "me-time". Or is it? So we can't necessarily drive off into the sunset, but that does not imply a perfect place for our meditation and prayer is not within reach. It may be as simple as a room in our home when things have quieted down for the day or a nearby place of worship when most people are not in attendance. Once we have found a comfortable location for our daily constitutional, the next aspect is preparing ourselves. This is extremely important for the success of our efforts. Consider the following steps.

Everything that happens in and around you is very important. Rest quietly and endeavor to expand your cognition to include what you are thinking, the emotions rising up in you, and what is affecting your senses like feeling, seeing, hearing, smelling, and tasting. Let each sensation happen to you and when it is finished let it go freely like a leaf floating away on a stream. Often this is quite enlightening as you realize how much you have been missing when you are so wrapped up in daily challenges.

Relax and be yourself. This could be that rare opportunity when you are not being judged or held up against impossible expectations. If you feel the people in your life have verbally or nonverbally communicated that you have not measured up to your potential, just let it go. What do they really know anyway? If you can't carry a tune in a basket but want to sing, do it. If you were told you have two left feet but want to dance, do it. If people shake their heads when they hear you talking to yourself, now you can do it without condemnation. If you want to talk to the Creator, you can do so without feeling ashamed or different.

Know this, you are not alone. You are awash with the love that permeates all things on our Earth Mother because they were made by the hand of God. Each tree, flower, bug and bear is a living being and so are you. Find peace in this knowledge. Let your mind empty itself out and let your tired body relax. If you fall asleep, so be it. This in no way implies the time has been wasted. An important style of talking to the Creator is called "praying in the spirit". That special essence found deep inside of you can communicate just as clearly as your mind or your lips and it will be heard. Be at home right here where you are and do not wish you were someone or someplace else. Now you are communicating with the Creator and, more importantly, listening.

* * * * * * * * *

A Quiet Place – Speaks

The brightly colored strands of fabric rippled in the bone chilling breeze. Red, yellow, black, white, and blue, easily eight feet long and six-inch wide ribbons of sail cloth fighting with the juniper bushes and the tangled knot restricting their freedom to fly away across the mountain side. Despite the gloomy and cloudy late afternoon in the Big Horn Mountains of Wyoming, the strands of cloth danced and twisted in a strangely gay profusion as if alive. A rainbow of colors cheerful and vibrant as they contrasted against the dull earth tones. There was no doubt in my mind, this was the place.

* * * * * * * * *

Had I continued to live with the Native people on Yakama Indian land in Washington State or in the Black Hills of South Dakota, I would have participated in this ritual called a "Vision Quest" during my early teen years. Now an overweight fifty year-old who has lived the "soft life" for at least half of those years, I was not looking forward with anticipation to the regimen before me.

So where will I go? Most acolytes seek a high place. I was unsure how to begin the steps toward warriorhood, so I met up with my friend, teacher, and mentor, Bobby "Medicine Grizzly Bear" Lake-Thom.

As we walked together, he began to counsel me, "At one time every tribe and band of Natives had sacred sites. Often, they were high places like caves, waterfalls, secret locations deep in the forest, or unusual geographical features. They were considered 'power centers' and special places for religious ceremonies, burials, training, and vision quests. Some were so sacred that only holy people dared go there. Some were so secret that complex ceremonies and rites had to be performed before entry could occur. All were marked or posted in some fashion to alert others to stay away. When the Europeans came, not only did they defile these sacred sites but they occasionally stole the markers. Today many of the old holy sites are lost or the people have been forced to move away from them. They will never be able to truly find themselves spiritually until they can return to their own sacred places. I think you should go to the Medicine Wheel."

"Never heard of it."

"It's in the Big Horn Mountains east of Yellowstone Park in Wyoming."

"I'll think about it. It's a long way from the Pacific Northwest where we live. Are there any closer places you can think of?"

No comment. You haven't lived until you see a Native American man roll his eyes and shake his head. It was becoming quite clear that no part of a vision quest is supposed to be convenient or easy for the participant.

My AAA road map of Wyoming showed the Medicine Wheel on Medicine Mountain at almost ten thousand feet of altitude in the middle of nowhere. I needed to find a safety net. It was too far to go when one could be injured or debilitated. I was willing to seek a vision, but I didn't want it to be a terminal activity. I called up my old high school friend Adam. He lived in Gillette, Wyoming. Yes, he would be willing to join me. He always wanted to explore the Medicine Wheel. He knew the rituals involving a vision quest. He was eager to help.

* * * * * * * * * *

The night before I headed east, the ceremony of purification in the turtle sweat lodge was exceptionally hot and oppressive. I had been in other sweat lodge rituals before, but never one so profound. The herbs and water hit the glowing lava rocks and splattered all over me. Suddenly superheated, I could feel the pain as blisters formed on my bare arms and shoulders. I gasped!

"You will need to be clean so the spirits will accept you," the Medicine Man informed me. "They are powerful. They could hurt you, even kill you. You need to be acceptable in the Creator's eyes."

I could not endure any more. I choked out the words of exit. "All my relations, please accept me into the Circle of Life."

It was good to get out of the sweat lodge and into the cold night air and the welcoming pond nearby where we could immerse ourselves. This one was a real pressure cooker. I felt weak and disoriented. My knees were rubbery and my breath did not satisfy the strangulated feeling in my throat and chest. The stars blurred and shimmered. My head ached.

* * * * * * * * *

I stopped eating after supper Sunday night. I must admit I loaded my plate a little more than usual. Until the fire ceremony the following Saturday evening, my fasting would involve ingesting only distilled water. Some ceremonial fasts also entail drinking juices and teas as well. Some of the elders say that water-only fasts weaken the psychic powers in a person. I was determined to do this the most difficult way. It had become a personal challenge.

"You will experience considerable discomfort in a day or so," explained Grizzly Bear. "If you can keep from eating during that time, your body will begin moving upward to the second plateau and will start living off its own body fat. You need to advance to the third level to be in the proper state for your vision. Push yourself."

My friend and I left from his home in eastern Wyoming and arrived at the Medicine Wheel mid-day Tuesday. It is the middle of August but the constant wind coursing over the bleak mountain ridge was biting and unwelcoming toward strangers. Grey, angry clouds marched eastward, unhampered by the snow-capped peaks around us. Splattering drops of rain left muddy footprints on my truck's windscreen. Occasional flashes of lightning and menacing thunder roll in from the west. This did not bode well at all.

The one lane asphalt road that left the main highway clings precariously to the side of the ridge, it twists and winds upward and northward over the top of the mountain. My anticipation heightened as I tried to picture in my mind what we would soon see. Once I decided on doing my vision quest there, I read some magazine articles on the setting and its mysteries. I envisioned some kind of American Indian Stonehenge waiting for me to behold.

We arrived at the parking area. No cars were allowed past the gate. It was a mile or so walk along the ridge to the Wheel. What a shock! There before me was a steel wire fence completely encircling what was left of the Medicine Wheel. Over the years, thoughtless people had been stealing the stones for souvenirs from the circular rock walls and from the spokes of rock rows that radiated toward the central altar. Other cairns of rocks marking a line with the summer solstice sunrise and sunset were picked away so much they are barely perceptible above ground-level. Off to the south of this sacred site, a huge air-traffic control radar dome hums angrily, a constant reminder to the spirits of the mountain that the White Man and his machines now rule the earth. I glanced toward the east rim of the fence and see medicine bundles, tobacco ties, feathers, bits of ribbon, and colorful cloth attached to the wire. Native people have honored the place with their prayer-ties despite the sacrilege. How appropriate. Before me in a simple microcosm was a parable relating the relationship between the Indigenous Peoples of this continent and those who have oppressed them. I turned away.

We picked our way north on the bare traces of a road along the ridge away from the Wheel until we found the colorful fabrics calling us to set up camp here. As the ensuing cold and windy days and long nights made themselves known, my friend was aware that I have to work myself toward exhaustion, so he pushes me. Each day was a new test. He observed that I was not tiring despite the lack of nourishment. We hike, we explore, we climb, and we pray. Each day is active and demanding, but I was able to keep up. He checks my eyes. Nights became fitful due to the dull ache in my stomach. So this is the emptiness that millions and millions of needy people across the planet experience every night of their difficult lives. As the light of day leaves us and darkness walks across the landscape, there are no lights except our dying campfire. No motors or signs at all, except for the cloth ribbons, that Man has walked here before us. I felt vulnerable and lonely despite the companionship of my friend. I did not realize just how noisy our daily lives are back in civilization. We have become so used to it we don't even notice.

The winds blow.

* * * * * * * * *

The time is approaching for the vision quest ceremony. This is my seventh day of fasting. I feel weak and unsteady and the temptation to put an end to all of this is quietly crawling into my thoughts. Someone or something doesn't want me to keep up the regimen. Maybe it's me.

As the blood red sun caresses the ragged mountain ranges to the west we begin preparations for the evening ceremonial fire. Tomorrow morning we must hike back down off the mountain and return to reality. This is our one and only chance. We clean out the fire pit and then I roll the first of several heavy rocks toward the fire area.

"What are you doing?" my friend inquires.

"I'm putting some large stones around the fire for the grandfather spirits to sit on. I want them to feel welcomed around our warm fire. I don't want them to have to sit on the wet ground."

"I'll help you. How many?"

"One for each of the Sacred Directions plus Father Sky and Mother Earth, six."

We stack whatever we can find for our campfire. Using the hand axe my friend brought, we were able to find firewood to burn during the week and still had a supply for our last campfire. There would be no man-made items in this fire. Everything must be as natural as possible. If I could start a fire without matches, I would. I hope the spirits will understand. The weather is turning colder. I can smell moisture on the wind again. A giant cloud bank is approaching from the northwest, grey fingers tinged with the redness of the disappearing sun reach out to claim the clear evening sky. Some stars briefly appear as if to say, "Goodbye. You will not see us much longer."

As darkness begins to master, the Great Horned Owls come, silent and angry. We are in their hunting grounds. They circle. They hunt. They approach then swerve away. Two of them are very large and foreboding. Possibly a male and female. Voiceless, they express their disapproval, "Two-leggeds, you have done enough to our earth. Hunting is hard. You have killed or frightened away our prey. Our children are starving. Leave us, leave us."

As our campfire dances brightly against the unfriendly darkness the ceremony begins. I sit facing the east, my friend the north. Despite the growing cold and dampness, our fire laughs at the night and touches us with its warm breath. I introduce myself in the correct manner and begin sprinkling ceremonial tobacco into the flames.

"Great Creator, Mother Earth, and all my relations, my name is Stan and my Native name is Ha-Gue-A-Dees-Sas. I come from Yakama Indian country. My race is part White and part Native. My nationality is American and this is why I am here. I am here on a vision quest. According to ancient customs and law, I feed you tobacco."

We chant an intonation of invitation to the Oo-kon'-nah-peh, the Grandfather Spirits.

"Grandfather Spirits who live in this place, please join us and warm yourselves around our fire. We have placed stones so you do not have to sit on the wet earth. We welcome your companionship and ask for your help and protection. We offer these gifts to you, sagebrush, tobacco, and cedar. We honor the sacred directions, East, South, West and North. We acknowledge Ah-teh'-mah-pe'-yah (Father Sky) and E-nah'-man-koh'-chay (Mother Earth)."

As I reach into the paper grocery bag of aromatic plants, I pull out a cloth scroll wrapped in gold ribbon. In the firelight I can see it is a letter from my little girl to the Children Spirits. A gift for the fire, a special touch for the magical night.

We wait expectantly, patiently. We humble ourselves and chant our prayers of penitence. Medicine Grizzly Bear calls this "Pah-gah'-soy."

We wait. Our fire becomes glowing coals and the mean winds pick up and chill our spirits. I can hear it whisper meanly, "No visions, no magic, no nothing. Lo-o-o-ser."

* * * * * * * * * * *

The first vestiges of rain approach as we silently break camp and prepare for the hike back to our vehicle. The sun is walking somewhere above the clouds, but there is no warmth around us. I no longer wonder why the earth is so barren on this ridge. The stunted juniper bushes seem to be able to resist the harshness of their environment and I admire them for that. Here and there are tufts of lodge grass holding onto the sparse earth behind piles of stones. What a strange place to construct a Medicine Wheel. Nobody would come up here, maybe that was the reason.

The brightly colored fabrics ripple in the cold breeze. Sacred colors: red, yellow, black, white, and blue. Indian people tied them there as a thanksgiving offering for allowing them to camp and pray. We leave some food, pour tea into the earth, and throw some tobacco into the wind. It is not much payment for spending five days on Holy Ground.

The return hike and later the drive off the mountain is silent, even pensive. Finally we share our disappointment, the rigors and commitment, the proper attitude, the expectations, and the correctness of the ceremonies but no visions.

We don't know when we will be able to find the time to try again.

OWLS – MASTERS OF THE NIGHT

Out of the black the Night Hunter came.
Silent and brooding - his eyes aflame.
I felt his hatred … a heavy cloud.
I heard his lament, but not said aloud.

"Two leggeds, you destroy everything.
You have frightened away my prey.
Hunting is hard. Our babies are starving.
Go away … go away … go away."

He circles around, his distain clear.
All he wanted was me out of there.
When he said "Who-o" it's easy to see
The cause of his pain … was me.

It's the owls who belong to the night.
Man lives in fear 'til returns the light.

PRESERVING A COMMUNITY OF FAITH

By the Waters of Babylon

"Why are we here, oh Toothless-one? My heart grows heavy. I don't like this at all."

"Silence, My-Child. Listen closely. Hear the wind sighing through the emptiness."

"Grandfather, I hear wailing. Some of the voices are very old. Why are they in torment?"

"They lament for the lost holy places."

"Tears are in my eyes, Old-One. What has happened?"

"In a young man's clothes, I once tried to worship in this place. When my feet were warm and a woman's eyes kindled my heart's embers. These stones stood one on another until we could not see Father-Sky. Glass of more colors than the rainbow reached out to

43

Grandfather-Sun and the fragrances, strange and exotic like a field of spring flowers.

"The singing … Ah, the singing. The angels wept for joy as the voices rose to Creator-God. My heart stirred, songs of triumph. Songs of celebration. Songs of pain and suffering. Songs of hope. Songs of longing and emptiness. Songs of praise and adoration… Where we are standing, the worshippers presented their offerings and partook in a sacred meal. That's why the ground is higher here."

"It sounds wonderful, My-Elder. Why is it all gone now?"

"Why? That *is* the question. Maybe like the elk fleeing the wolf they grew tired. Maybe they forgot why they walked the Earth-Mother and defiled her. Maybe like a Tribe with many summers of good gathering they became too comfortable. Voices warned them. Their prophets' words were written on the stone walls in runes not to be ignored. The warnings said simply: 'Don't rest on the accomplishments of the past'.

"I don't understand, Grandfather."

"The villages and clans of the Old-Ones were there for replenishment and comfort, but they failed to understand that their calling was to also touch the tears of all human beings. The houses of worship were the central settings within which people were encountered and embraced by the gentle touch of God. In the writings, the ceremonies and mission the gathered community of faith became God's will on earth, living and loving, suffering and redeeming, dying and rising again in the new world waiting for the faithful. Each member of the worshiping community was called to be open and vulnerable to the pains and cries of all God's people and to be part of the world's healing.

"As I tried to become a member of their family it became clear to me that everyone was looking in and not looking out. I came to them, hungry for their Sacred Writings and the wisdom of their Holy Men. I longed to join their beautiful songs and liturgies. But, they turned away from me. I found myself sitting in the back of their beautiful temples, alone. Some seemed concerned about my pain and brokenness but they were not heard. They were met with resistance and isolation and I felt small and unclean. All I could do was walk away in tears."

"Is that why it is all gone now, Grandfather?"

"Yes, the prophets stood in the High Places and told them what needed to be done. But their cries fell on closed ears. Once they numbered like stones in the earth when we prepare our land for the corn planting. Each as the other in mind and spirit unwilling to open their souls to the needs of so many others. My heart truly aches when I think about their demise."

"Grandfather, could we return to our village? It's cold here."

"I was cold then also, My-Child. Let us go home."

* * * * * * * * * *

Seek and Ye Shall Find – The Art of Welcoming

"I want to be like you."

His Native American grandparents called him "Cries for Ribs", but he told everybody his name was Cletus Stoddard. He was one of the better students in my elementary school classroom. I was his teacher. Cletus was very artistic and athletic and he had that ability to get along with just about anybody. I especially appreciated his gifts and talents and tried to establish situations where he could put them to use. I truly sensed the light of God in his eye which is not that uncommon in young children.

He occasionally stayed after class was dismissed to help tidy-up the room and visit awhile. One spring day as we chatted about nothing in general, he looked up at me and said simply, "Mr. Hughes, when I grow up, I want to be just like you."

I was flattered and responded that being a teacher was not easy. The pay was not very good and it took a long time to get trained, the normal litany of teacher woes. I did encourage him that with his abilities and personality he could be anything he wanted to be and that the world could always use another good teacher. He looked at me pensively for a moment then he continued his tasks and eventually left for the day.

It was a long time later that I realized Cletus was not thinking about being a teacher. As he stated, he wanted to be like me. I had something of value that he felt and that he longed for. I have often thought about what that something of value was and I think it was my sense of belonging and a willingness to share that peace with the people who were around me.

Could this be the very heart of those who worship God in any religion? This could be a special motivator for us to reach out to our disenfranchised brothers and sisters. How rich the harvest would be if we let them know as believers in our particular faith that we truly have something of real value.

What are the spiritual commitments of the general North America population? Studies have shown that about thirty to forty percent are willing to identify themselves as Protestant, Catholic, Mormon, or another "main" Christian denomination. Another fifteen percent or so embrace expression of faiths not normally associated with Euro-American based religions. That leaves up to half of our brothers and sisters in this country with no formal expression of faith at all. Acres and acres ready for the harvesters.

Are there any common traits among the uncommitted that we should be aware of? These are generalities and, of course, do not apply to everyone. People who are not interested in joining an organized religion may have had an unpleasant religious experience sometime in their lives either as children or adults. I.e. the nun with the yardstick, a parent making them attend on a regular basis, an abusive religious leader demanding and unyielding to the needs of others, acquaintances who were judgmental and aloof toward them, or others holding up their wealth and happiness making people feel inferior or inadequate.

Another reason might be the attitude held by the intellectual elite that Creationism is just propaganda and Evolution explains everything, so attributing anything to God is trite and primitive. We should not underestimate the effects of social media. People are looking down at their toys and not up. They feel satisfied by the anonymity of the internet and feel empowered to do and say whatever they feel without being held responsible for their actions. It seems many of these people have a linear sense of life. You are born, you live, you die, and then you are a smorgasbord for the worms.

In today's world, it might just be an issue of time. Americans are on the run day in and day out, trying to make ends meet and trying to address the needs of themselves and their families. If they can collect some quality time for themselves and their families, then attending a religious service is well down the list of things being considered.

Believers in all faiths realize that they truly do have something of value to offer their brothers and sisters. So how can we reap this incredibly rich harvest? Let us first look at an example of reaping close to home of what did not work.

When the Europeans began to dominate this continent, they brought with them a philosophy of linear development and progress-oriented effort. In the Caribbean, when the Native population died off from disease and deprivation, they were replaced by African slaves. The slave trade proved to be so lucrative that it expanded onto the continent, mainly in southeastern United States. When the American West's great railroad building boom of the mid- and late 1800's emerged, Asian workers were imported to do the back-breaking toil. When the railroads were completed, thousands of laborers were left to their own devices if they could not return home. They became victims of the dominant society and were considered unworthy of what the American Dream promised Euro-Americans. Unable to secure protection from government institutions, they cloistered themselves into closed communities. Almost every large western American city has a Chinatown. In every case, these immigrants were considered property rather than people and were treated worse than livestock.

The original inhabitants of North America were persecuted, bullied, and mistreated. In a painfully short period of time they were emasculated, belittled, and forced onto reservations. The United States government made them sign treaties even though their leaders could neither read nor write. (See a sample of a treaty in Appendix 1). Their ancestral lands, which they had utilized for countless generations, were divided up into parcels and either sold or given to the members of the dominant society.

The African, Asian, and Native populations generally perceived their world with the idea of cyclical re-affirmation and that peace and prosperity was measured by achieving harmonious balance with Self-Others-Nature-God (SONG). This tenet was called "Circle of Life". The Euro-American influence both directly and indirectly infringed upon the cultural and spiritual components of these displaced people. Enjoying the role as the Dominant Society, they ridiculed those whose skin was not white and made them feel embarrassed and ashamed about their time-honored beliefs. They were shocked and confused as a result of these attacks and began to carry a great yoke of pain on their backs. This pain which so many of them endure even today emanates from intentional and unintentional messages from the dominant culture's institutions of government, economics, and, sadly, the church.

This deep-seated pain which still consumes so many people who feel disenfranchised by the American Dream is reflected in the formation of gangs, violence, chemical dependency, family dysfunction, a sense of hopelessness, and suicide. In treatment programs serving these people, we are told that the most difficult issues in recovery are getting re-connected spiritually, physically, emotionally, and mentally. Beneath a façade of hostility and anger in many of those on the outside looking in lurks the fear that somehow, because one is not white-skinned, he or she is permanently excluded from the good things society has to offer. Imagine how devastating it is to feel that you can never measure up in society. Now join this feeling with the deep-seated fear that you are an outcast in the eyes of God and you are closer to truly understanding the dilemma in the hearts and souls of too many people turned off by organized religion of any kind.

Armed with this new understanding, we can now walk into the various cultures that decorate our nation and say sincerely, "You are my brothers and sisters and we are all equal in the eyes of God."

* * * * * * * * *

The Pillars of our Beliefs and our Efforts to Share Them
"My heart is open, please feed me."

Now the work begins. As harvesters it is imperative, despite our particular faiths, to communicate what we believe and how it might help the people demonstrating even the slightest interest in what we have to offer. Listed below are just a few of the common tenets to think about:

Here and the Hereafter - This is a very difficult concept to communicate and might be one to talk about sometime after we have developed some form of positive ongoing contact with the potential member. Many North Americans are so wrapped up in the here and now that any concern for the future, except where will the next meal come from, crumbles under the pressure of present needs, comforts, and desires. Religious leaders have to work diligently to keep their own members, as well as new people, thinking about what lies ahead, preparing for the inevitable, and saving for a rainy day. For those who are not yet committed to our efforts, paradise somewhere off in the future that is beyond thought or understanding is just a word in the dictionary. The paradise we discuss might be a garden of earthly delights or a place of peace and fulfillment. In all cases it represents an improvement in the human condition and is worth looking forward to.

Life and Death - We talked earlier about the general idea about life for many unbelievers. Simply you are born, you live as long as you can, and then you die. Period. While alive you endeavor to make it as comfortable and as successful as possible, realizing that in the end, unless you have provided for your family, it was all to no avail. This lack of appreciation or even lack of fear for the death event often predicates people doing death-defying activities just for the thrill of it. Some become casual and careless with their lives which leads to self-destructive activities like chemical abuse, violence, gang membership, and suicide. Religious leaders who try to communicate that the human body is the temple of God and should be cared for experience their efforts falling on deaf ears, especially if the body of the listener does not measure up to what is considered desirable or at least optimal.

<u>Time</u> - An important tenet of the major faiths in our country deals with the concept of time. Being punctual and time conscious is considered a virtue and important to the interchange of goods and ideas. All the faiths serving in our nation work on strict timetables: Minutes, hours, days, and weeks. Everyone's holy year is laid out with special messages, colors, and ceremony spread over the twelve months. Those considering becoming members of the family may be confused as these events unfold and as their importance is communicated. I remember the story of a young man who had spent a number of years in a refugee camp in central Africa. As each agonizing day crawled across the landscape, there was no reason to keep track of time. In fact it made it somewhat more bearable to just concentrate on breathing. When he was repatriated and returned to a more normal existence he had a difficult time adjusting to having to be someplace at some special time.

<u>In the Beginning</u> - Lost in the present day diatribes of two major religions demeaning each other is the inspirational story of Abraham, Sarah, and Hagar. Few religious leaders these days seem to want to share the idea that ancient history tells us that Islam and Judeo-Christianity emerged from the same seed. Islam through Hagar and Ishmael and Judeo-Christianity through Sarah and Isaac. When the glorious day comes when they are looking for commonalities rather than differences, this story would be a great place to start. The beautiful poetry of the major religions' sacred writings includes in their creation stories show the closeness of God to humankind. His hand touches his children and a most gentle father-son relationship develops. This crashes violently with those who "poo-poo" these creation stories and embrace the theory of evolution and refuse to even discuss the situation. People who simply do not believe in God spend little time wondering how it all began.

Prophets and Speakers of the Truth - Most communities of faith have people who historically were touched by the hand of the Creator and were charged with bringing His message to the believers. Whether they are called prophets, saints, angels, heavenly beings, or some other descriptive word they were and still are important members of the religious hierarchy. I believe sharing the works and the writings of these holy people with those who may be considering becoming a part of the family allows all of us to understand more clearly that humans are an integral part of the ideology and that we are charged with receiving and passing on the messages of how to live and how to strive to become better.

Rites and Rituals - The elder Native in the beginning of this story told his grandson how entering the temple of God touched the senses.

"Glass of more colors than the rainbow reached out to Grandfather-Sun and the fragrances, strange and exotic like a field of spring flowers. The singing, ah, the singing. The angels wept for joy as the voices rose to Creator God…"

The ceremonies of the major religions were developed over the centuries and now reach out to the believers like guiding hands. Each of the senses is touched and magnified, pointing the participant into the flow of the worship. There is a comfortable feeling of continuity and belonging in knowing that the words and music embracing you have been spoken and sung beyond memory. As someone enters the house of worship for the first time it is not unusual for that person to be swept up in the rites and rituals and want to experience more. Not surprising that some confusion may arise about the significance of what is going on. Consider the dialog from a Native elder named George Nicotine:

Me and My Many Baptisms
My father used to tell me that I was a no-good Indian and
he was determined to make a good Indian out of me. So he

put me in a Catholic Church school. They told me they had to baptize me. So they did and named me "David". I had not known that David was the giant killer.

So, I was known as David, which lasted about three months and then my dad had to move to a new job, so I had to go to a new school. That meant new teachers and staff. Again, they said we will have to baptize you. So they went through the ceremony and named me "John". I did not know that the name John meant "dragon slayer".

I really felt like I had grown up in the past four months. My dad worked two months and was transferred to another job some eighty miles away from the last school. Again I was approached by a minister who said that I must be baptized again. Again I went through the ceremony. This time I was named "Peter." When I grew up I realized that the name "Peter" was the name that meant I was in charge of the key to the Pearly Gates.

Talking to God - Man's ability to communicate with the Creator is a significant pillar of faith in all major religions. What do we pray for and how do we do it? Can we classify prayer depending upon the purpose or theme? Looking at prayer from this somewhat academic point of view, it becomes apparent how versatile and important prayer really can become. Thinking about prayers I have read, heard, or recited, they seem to fall into at least some of the following categories.

Praise and adoration – It is right and salutatory to praise the Creator and to tell Him how much we love Him. Someone told me one time He likes to hear from us in this way.

<u>Intercession</u> – We all know friends and loved ones who do not pray nor even believe. In their isolation and loneliness, we uplift them to the Holy One so He will not forget their names.

<u>Petition and solicitation</u> – It is okay to ask Him for things and for a better life. Historical faith writings reinforce two important issues. God does indeed listen and knows our hearts desires before we ask and He can have his mind changed by our pleading.

<u>Protection and help</u> – As long as people have believed in God, they have petitioned Him to deliver them from the "Valley of Death" or from the hands of their enemies. In these present times we may not necessarily be in danger for our lives, but we still need help from on high for health and economic issues. The world of today is fraught with pitfalls and it is almost impossible to make it through them without someone to lean on.

<u>Thanksgiving, gratitude and joy</u> – "Not by my hand, but yours." We come into the world helpless, toothless, and naked. We will leave this vale of tears helpless, toothless, and naked. All good things come from the Creator and he has promised that we will be able to handle the bad things.

<u>Healing</u> – Our Father understands the toll illnesses take on His people. Miracles are happening every day by His hand. A friend of mine was diminishing from a very serious malady. Whether or not it was His will, the end was inevitable. In my grief, she reminded me not to confuse "wellness with wholeness". She was leaving with no regrets and looking forward to the next adventure.

<u>Prayers of imprecation</u> – invoking God's judgement on the wicked.

Repentance – We are human and we make mistakes, on purpose or by accident, in thought, words, and deeds done and undone. If we are sorry and promise to not continue the activities we will be forgiven. Thank God for that!

There is marvelous comfort and a sense of belonging when someone actually realizes that the most powerful entity of all is there listening and caring. All one needs to do is believe. As my grandmother aged and weakened over the years, she told me she could always pray for her family and our country. She told me that she would go to sleep praying and wake up still praying. This was an example of what is called "praying in the spirit".

Tithing and Benevolence - All the good things might tumble on down on us, but we have a responsibility also. Every major religion professes that the blessed show an appreciation for the good things they are receiving by giving back. It might be ten percent of a crop or actual income or it might be as small as "the widow's mite". The point is, you give all you can of your money, your time, and your commitment and graciously.

Grace and Redemption - To those who embrace a faith, grace and redemption basically mean that despite our human weaknesses God sees our worth and value and does not give up on us. This is a difficult concept to grasp when we begin to realize the hurtful, thoughtless, and unkind things we have done or left undone during our lives. Some Native groups believe a loving Creator is waiting for us to return to His arms, but we must *peh-gah-soy* (repent) for our shortcomings. To know there is hope for us after all is so comforting when we are surrounded by people in our lives who have given up on us or when we have given up on ourselves. This may be one of the most important blessings we can share with the newcomer. The baggage people carry in their lives can be so heavy it bends them over. Here is an opportunity to let them stand up straight and stride forward with confidence and humility.

* * * * * * * * * *

Conserving the New Members

"I gave it a try a couple times. It didn't do anything for me."

Why do worshippers leave the fold? The answers are as varied as those departing, but it may be helpful to place them into categories:

Priorities - Life is difficult. The demands on the people of the twenty-first century are as laborious as in any time in recent history. It is harder and harder to make a living and support a family. Each person has a finite amount of energy to keep up and they must prioritize their efforts and commitments. By the weekend, many just want to stay home and watch football or the Home and Garden Channel. They say simply, "It's not important enough to me to keep me attending. I'd rather be doing something else with what little time is mine."

Social Interaction Issues - In any group of people, even faithful people, personalities do not always blend smoothly. Even the most trivial issues can raise people's hackles. Attend a meeting to discuss next year's budget and see the camps form. Listen to the conversation around the coffee pot, "I don't like ___ and ___ doesn't like me." Fill in the blanks. Newbies are especially vulnerable as they are pulled back and forth by those endeavoring to strengthen their positions. We profess we are brothers and sisters in faith and unfortunately we sometimes act like real brothers and sisters.

Doctrinal or Liturgical - Each community of faith has developed its own ways of professing the Word over the years. That doctrine is presented to the new member and he or she is primed to receive it and accept it and to fit in. New member classes help people understand expectations. After exposure to the rites, rituals, and the needed disciplines, the novices may decide it is not feeding their hunger. Some people are 'church shopping' and they are unwilling to stay with it for a while to really understand what the true message is.

<u>Situations Beyond Their Control</u> - People who leave but really don't want to are the ones most heartfelt. Changing jobs, the break-up of marriages, extended illness, the factors are almost endless. There really isn't any recourse except to send them off with prayers, good wishes, a promise to keep them in our hearts, and a reminder that the welcome mat is always out for them should they come home.

* * * * * * *

The new person being welcomed into the fold experiences the spiritual ebbs and flows that everyone else has. When they first have that born-again experience the flames burn brightly because of the newness and promise, the sense of equality and community is uplifting as well as comforting. Many begin to feel enabled for the first time, empowered "to do" and "to be". Then reality sets in. Keeping the fires burning takes hard work. Not all of their new brothers and sisters are generous, helpful, or sensitive to other's differences. Not all old-timers welcome strangers warmly and openly. There may even be members that the new person knows who definitely do not represent in the work-a-day world the good things a religion has to offer.

It is discouraging to realize that sometimes the person who "harvested" the fledgling convert moves on to new fields, assuming that the new member is now fixed and can grow on his or her own just by participating in the life of the community of faith. A new member may have developed a trust and comfort with the person who found him or her and expect that person will continue to be at hand to reach out to. However, as often as not it is expected that others will accept the responsibility for conserving this infant believer. He or she will be signed up to participate in new member classes, sometimes this is actually mandated, and then a sense of school becomes associated with the church. The new member receives his or her first copy of the sacred writings and is left to somehow read it and learn all its knowledge. Thousands of pages of tiny print are, at the very least, very overwhelming. So, classes are offered and more sense of school emerges. Even more perplexing the new member may look around his new surroundings and realize nobody else looks like him.

To conserve our fledgling converts we must develop the support system needed to constantly reinforce that his or her participation is valued and needed, just like we should do for all of our people:

1. Identify a mentor that is willing to walk with and guide the novice and not just during worship times.
2. Find his or her interests and build upon them. One of the greatest evangelism and conservation programs in modern times might be the Jack and Jill softball team.
3. Allow him or her to participate in the Service of the Word on equal footing as opportunities provided for ongoing members of the community of faith
4. Arrange home visits to meet in the comfort of the familiar surroundings of the fledgling. This needs to be the choice of the new member since there are countless reasons to not open one's home to others. Inversely, people should be willing to invite the novice into their homes in a social setting. This would be a great time to initiate a progressive dinner.
5. Potlucks and other communal events held at the place of worship should include a personal invitation and possibly trans-

portation to and from. It should be clear that the invitation is for the whole family.

6. New people imply new needs. Community of faith leaders need to find out the specific concerns of their postulant and address them and provide resolutions within their abilities.

7. And more important than any other issue, the brand new member should never feel isolated nor feel that the only reason his or her presence is wanted is to bring more money and resources into the fold or to fill some quota requirement.

It will take the person-to-person touch to keep the new members. It will take understanding and consideration to allow his or her experiences to be positive and nurturing. It will take hard work and constant reinforcement in order that the novice will choose to continue participating. Believers will have to prove to the fledgling that not only is there a place for them but their uniqueness and abilities are needed as well.

Human theology is not static. Each worshipper is called to a vital engagement with the written words of his faith to discern God and his prophets' will for our actions in history. Our hierology understandings, our policies and practices, and even our values and world view need to be open to critique, reshaping, and renewing. We need to be open to the transforming work of the sacred writings as they speak to our hearts. Sometimes God will speak through the lives of others, the person who is the stranger in our midst, the person who is hungry, the person of a different race.

Church Leaders' Apology – One of the Most Thoughtful Actions Nobody Remembers

From the clouds of over thirty years ago, a most marvelous voice still calls to the people of this troubled nation. Could it be this sacred song now falls on deaf ears?

A Public Declaration to the Tribal Councils and Traditional Spiritual Leaders of the Indian and Eskimo Peoples of the Pacific Northwest.

Dear Brothers and Sisters,

This is a formal apology on behalf of our churches for their long-standing participation in the destruction of traditional Native American spiritual practices. We call upon our people for recognition of and respect for your traditional ways of life and for protection of your sacred places and ceremonial objects. We have frequently been unconscious and insensitive and not come to your aid when you have been victimized by unjust Federal policies and practices. In many other circumstances we reflected the rampant racism and prejudice of the dominant culture with which we too willingly identified. We, as leaders of our churches in the Pacific Northwest, extend our apology. We ask for your forgiveness and blessing.

As the Creator continues to renew the earth, the plants, the animals, and all living things, we call upon the people of our denominations and fellowships to a commitment of mutual support in your efforts to reclaim and protect the legacy of your own traditional spiritual teachings. To that end we pledge our support and assistance in upholding the American Religious Freedom Act (P.L.95-134, 1978) and within that legal precedent affirm the following:

1. The rights of the Native Peoples to practice and participate in traditional ceremonies and rituals with the same protection offered all religions under the Constitution.

2. Access to and protection of sacred sites and public lands for ceremonial purposes.

3. The use of religious symbols (feathers, tobacco, sweet grass, bone, etc.) for use in traditional ceremonies and rituals.

The spiritual power of the land and the ancient wisdom of your indigenous religion can be, we believe, great gifts to the Christian churches. We offer our commitment to support you in the righting of previous wrongs; to protect your peoples' efforts to enhance Native spiritual teachings; to encourage the members of our churches to stand in solidarity with you on these important issues; to provide advocacy and mediation, when appropriate, for ongoing negotiations with State agencies and Federal officials regarding these matters.

May the promises of this day go on public record with all the congregations of our communions and be communicated to the Native American Peoples of the Pacific Northwest. May the God of Abraham and Sarah, and the Spirit who lives in both the Cedar and Salmon People, be honored and celebrated.

Sincerely,

The Rev. Thomas L. Blevins, Bishop
Pacific Northwest Synod –
Lutheran Church in America

The Rev. Dr. Ralph Bradford
Executive Minister
American Baptist Churches of the
Northwest

The Rev. Robert Brock
N.W. Regional Christian Church

The Right Rev. Robert H. Cochrane
Bishop, Episcopal Diocese of Olympia

The Rev. W. James Halfaker
Conference Minister
Washington North Idaho Conference
United Church of Christ

The Most Rev. Raymond G.
Hunthausen
Archbishop of Seattle
Roman Catholic Archdiocese of
Seattle

The Rev. Elizabeth Knott
Synod Executive
Presbyterian Church
Synod Alaska-Northwest

The Rev. Lowell Knutson
Bishop
North Pacific District
American Lutheran Church

The Most Rev. Thomas Murphy
Coadjutor Archbishop
Roman Catholic Archdiocese of Seattle

The Rev. Melvin G. Talbert, Bishop
United Methodist Church
Pacific Northwest Conference

Our Hope for Peace –
Finding our Warriors

Looking over the history of the United States, a case could be made to support the idea that we are the Spartans of the modern age. Students of the topic claim that of the last 242 years since the Revolutionary War our nation has been engaged in some form of combat either at home or abroad for 225 of those years. Does the modern-day warrior class of Sparta now walk the North American continent? Consider the following premises.

<u>Who and what do we celebrate</u>: Take a look at any calendar. Almost every month has some warrior or conflict-related holiday being observed somewhere in our country. Just an overview:

January 8 – the Battle of New Orleans

February 15 – President's Day (think how many of our Presidents had military backgrounds).

March 15 – General Andrew Jackson's birthday.

April 19 – Patriot's Day.

May 10 – Confederate's Memorial Day

May 30 – National Memorial Day

June 14 – Flag Day

July 4 – National Independence Day

August 16 – Battle of Bennington

September 12 – Defender's Day

November 11 – Veteran's Day

…and this barely scratches the surface of military-related ceremonies celebrated from coast to coast.

Consider the toys our children play with: G.I. Joe dolls, plus his friends and enemies, have been on the shelves of toy stores for over thirty years. The military equipment used by Joe would be the envy of almost every third-world country. Squirt guns are now squirt rifles that extoll new technology fire power and shooting distances. Kung-fu weapons, although plastic and wood replicas, are in most boy's bedrooms not to mention how many Kung-Fu, Taekwondo, and other Asian martial arts classes are offered for children as young as four years old. Video games and arcades are more and more realistic as children kill and maim their way to higher and higher scores. Laser tag activity centers are springing up across our nation, providing socially acceptable outlets for people to "shoot" each other. Toy guns are so realistic that they have brought about injury and death to children and adults at the hands of law enforcement officers who were, understandably, thinking they were in mortal danger. They litter the closets and carpets of many American homes. Kids still play Cowboys and Indians, pretending to shoot each other to death. And the story goes on…

<u>Consider our economy</u>: War brings jobs and new weaponry. The rusting wheels of American industry, too stagnated to find creative and uplifting ways to improve our lives, now hum and click noisily as they crank out articles of destruction. Drones as large as airplanes fly the skies loaded with alarming weaponry seeking out real or imagined enemies being piloted by a warrior hundreds, if not thousands, of miles away from the targets. Computers and technology are programmed to bring pain and death to the people they are pointed at. American workers tally and pack the instruments of war, not realizing how dehumanizing it is to their spirits and not understanding they are indirectly as responsible as the person who pulls the trigger.

* * * * * * * * * *

When we conjure up an image of a warrior, normally it is a strong young man in military dress armed to the teeth and ready for action or some kind of muscular super hero from the movies brandishing a sword and fighting evil. But, is this truly the complete picture? Can a warrior be an aged person, a child, a physically challenged person or a woman engaged in an action designed to better the lives or the safety of people counting on them?

Let us look deeper into the issue and consider the criteria for warrior-hood long-established in traditional Native American lore.

A warrior has, at the center of his or her being, a sense of caring and protection. This passion sustains the warrior against any challenges.

To be truly valued, the warrior must be seen in the larger context of society. His or her role may vary from culture to culture depending on necessity, responsibilities, traditions, and expectations.

The unguided warrior who is consumed by the passion of battle rather than hopeful outcomes is a destroyer. A warrior is valued when his or her heart beats for the protection of the larger whole and his or her motivations are good.

True warrior's courage comes from loving those depending upon him or her and a willingness to put those people before him or herself.

If we consider these criteria, our image of a warrior is dramatically changed. Put away the camo clothing and weaponry and uplift those people in our community willing to put all on the line for the betterment of each of us.

* * * * * * * * * *

Do we really appreciate the warriors these days and what they were trying to accomplish?

While at the American Indian Community Center in Spokane, Washington, I was visiting with someone who might be considered an old warrior who had been at Wounded Knee, South Dakota in the early 1970's when members of the Sioux nation and the U.S. government went eye-to-eye over many critical issues of self-determination. I was saddened when he lamented how little those brave people are now appreciated for the price they had to pay personally as well as economically. Today, those warriors who endeavored to stand up against the F.B.I. are considered by some as radicals and fanatics and are accused of setting back interracial relations. He talked about how this new generation of young people do not care, nor even remember, much about what happened. He felt the American Indians of today have it pretty good and can count on peace and much more support and sensitivity from the dominant culture and they are unwilling to admit they have gained these benefits at the costs paid by earlier warriors.

I reflected over his pain for a long time. I could not comment personally because I was not there fighting for the rights of American Indians. I had been assimilated into the dominant culture for years, rested comfortably in a pleasant life style and, frankly, I showed little patience for those people at Wounded Knee and the turmoil I felt they were causing.

As time went by I found myself mulling over the words of the old warrior. I had a revelation that I wished I could have shared with him. Was this not the true repayment for a warrior's efforts? To know that the next generation has a better chance to enjoy peace and prosperity because of the ground broken by their efforts. I hope that old warrior can someday realize how things have improved and rest peacefully in the knowledge that he did his job and did it well.

OLD WARRIOR

My bite was of an angry wolf.
My teeth were white and strong.
My feathers were like river rocks,
Each one my right hand won.
My enemies fell on their knees
And cried in their defeat.
They broke their bows and tomahawks
And placed them at my feet.
Now I watch our brave young men
Riding off to war.
The maidens chant their farewell songs
Of long remembered lore.
My knees are stiff, my teeth are gone,
My eyes no longer keen.
No one seems to know my face,
So seldom is it seen.
Mighty, mighty great in war I was honored.
Now behold me old and wretched
Ha-Gue-A-Dees-Sas

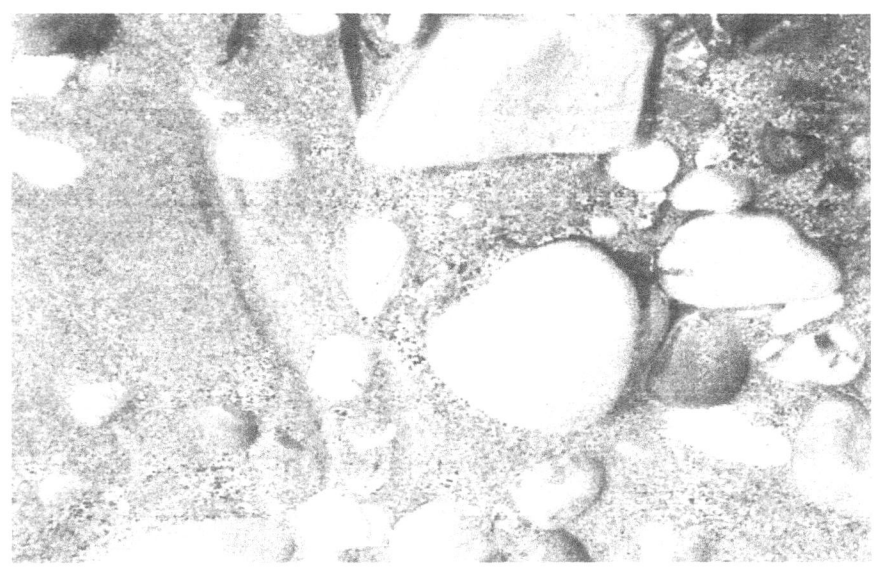

A Prayer in Your Pocket –
Finding Your *Watai*

Maybe the Pet Rock craze of 1975 wasn't so nuts after all.

* * * * * * * * * *

Traditional American Indians saw Creator God's touch in all aspects of their temporal environment. His handiwork was not just with the people and animals but in normally construed inanimate objects such as mountains, rainbows, rivers, stars, trees, and strangely rocks.

Some Northern Plains traditional natives share a legend that somewhere, in possibly the least expected location, a *watai* (stone) is waiting for the person whose spiritual journey is taking them from the distractions and trifles of the modern world back to the earth and simpler times. This is a special rock among the billions scattered across the face of Mother Earth. It contains a personal message for that person, a stone silently waiting since the dawn of time and marked by the Great Spirit with medicine, power, wisdom, and truth for each of us.

* * * * * * * * * *

My *watai* came to me attached to a necklace of leather with old Hudson's Bay Reds and silver trading beads attached. It is a four-inch long quartz crystal given to me by an Indian shaman (Medicine Man) in response to a number of years of kindnesses offered to him and his family. The shaman wove a story of the stone. Very ancient, it grew in the womb of the Earth Mother. Eons later, a Lemurian holy man harvested it with appropriate ceremony and used it for healing and communication purposes. Lemuria was America's west coast equivalent of Atlantis and in legend was covered by the ocean off what is now called California. My special rock was passed down through the ages and was utilized in rites and rituals. Its holders did good with the stone and it was always a blessing to those who came in contact with it. The shaman attested this was the story the *watai* told him.

When he presented the crystal to me, it was almost as clear as glass. Close inspection disclosed some rainbows if the stone was held just right in the sunlight. It felt good to hold it and seemed to help me center myself when I felt the need to pray for someone or something. Over the years, the crystal has begun to get colorless wisps and feathery shapes throughout the interior. I inquired to the Medicine Man as to what was happening. His response was that my special gift was taking on all my illnesses and impurities. This would insure a long and healthy life. Later, I showed the stone to a geologist friend who teaches at a nearby university. He marveled at the crystal from his scientific point of view. His explanation for the feathering was that all rocks have microscopic cracks and fissures, including quartz crystals. Water vapor eventually works into these faults and becomes visible. He suggested putting the cut end in sea salt and keeping it in a warm place for a few days. This would draw out the water and return it to its original condition. I liked the shaman's explanation. I kept the *watai* for over thirty years and enjoyed a life of health and happiness. I gifted it to my older granddaughter recently when she joined the U.S. Marine Corps. It is my hope it will continue to protect her as it did me.

* * * * * * * * * *

When I was a school principal, one of my primary grade teachers took her students outside to scour the playground for rocks to use for a counting and sorting mathematics exercise. She instructed the children concerning the size of the stones to be collected so the lesson would not become a boulder sorting drill. As she too collected samples for the project, she found one that looked like it had been split in half, rounded on one side and flat-surfaced on the other. Inspecting the stone, the exposed flat surface was a beige color with an impression of a gray arrowhead centered on the tan field. Remembering my Native heritage and interest in artifacts she placed it in her pocket to give to me later in the day.

I accepted the gift with interest and later tried to rub-off the arrowhead image, wondering who would color on a rock. It appeared to have been drawn and shaded-in with some kind of felt marker. Despite hot water and detergent, and later rubbing alcohol, the design remained intact and was now more vividly contrasted because the rest of the stone surface was clean. I kept the stone on my desk for some time then passed it on to one of my grandsons as part of a treasure box of interesting items for one of his Christmas presents. Inspecting the contents, he was immediately drawn to the unusual rock and studiously observed what he had found then he placed it in his pocket for further inspection.

He told me sometime later that the rock "talks to him" so he keeps it with his "good stuff." I think he has found his *watai*.

* * * * * * * * * *

My friend Ron thought he had found his *watai* while wandering in the deserts of the state of Arizona. His was a flat, oval-shaped stone, gray and no more than three or four inches across. An ancient symbol of a spider had been incised upon it. Clearly it was very old, as are all rocks, and it may have been used ceremonially. He kept it in his pocket for many years wrapped in a deerskin cloth and he used it as an earthly element for praying and meditation. It was pleasant to hold in his hand and served as a concentration point. One evening we were having dinner together and he claimed the stone was bringing him messages from the Star People (the *Woh'-geh*). He was being instructed to travel to the northwest Pacific coast until he found a "high place" that he would recognize, wait there for two nights, and the Star People would rendezvous with him.

All my conventional rationale offered to him about how strange that message was fell on deaf ears. So I asked him the most important question, "What happens if you do everything and nothing happens?"

He reflected a moment, then replied, "Well, I guess I'll come back and get a job and just be Ron."

Some days later he was back in town and told me a story of disappointment. There was no meeting with the Star People. In fact he injured himself climbing down the mountainside in the dark. During his tumble his *watai* had cracked in two, so in disgust he cast it into a nearby stream. I do believe in the power of these special stones so I still wonder about just what happened. Maybe he was projecting a deep-seated wish onto his artifact and failed to realize the source of the message was himself.

* * * * * * * * *

If we can embrace the idea that somewhere the *watai* given to each of us by the Creator is waiting to be discovered, how does this change our perception of the world around us? Most certainly we become more appreciative of our environment and a little less eager to dig, bulldoze, excavate, and pave over everything. Imagine God's exasperation if he knows that we buried the special gift he made for us under a concrete slab we were planning to put our new hot tub on. Even if it was crying out to us, its voice would be muffled forever.

Have you found your *watai* yet? If not, I believe you will know it innately when you do. Robert O'Rourke, a Colorado writer and folk artist, found his "… not on a sacred prairie but in a noisy city parking lot. An orphan, so out of place there." Just a humble rock laying there patiently waiting for the glorious reunion. Keep your eyes and heart open. It will be marvelous.

BASKET WOMAN'S ACT OF LOVE

At first, they rise from Mother Earth
Open their eyes and seek the sun.
Their arms stretched out in painless birth.
Awaiting the touch of the One
Who can foretell their future worth.

The Weaver picks the very best.
Her eyes can see what will become.
They soon will be her special guest.
Soft and smooth t'ween finger and thumb.
Brothers alike they gently rest.

She splays them out and makes a plan.
Her mind can see the finished rows.

The reeds themselves guide her soft hands.
Before her eyes the child grows.
Embraced as one, more than a strand.

Row on row, around and around.
Through and over, back and again.
It slowly rises from the ground
Never asking, "What might have been?"
Only won'dring, "Where am I bound?"

Now satisfied, she eyes her art.
Each reed holds tight to his brother.
They know they're just a single part
Of the love of their new Mother.
A manifest of her warm heart.

Just a simple basket? Look deeper.

DEATH BE NOT PROUD

Religious communities deal with the concept of death in ways as varied as those cultures differ from each other. And, to make it even more complicated, within each grouping different social strata, families, and individuals respond to death in unique ways. However, it is possible to classify all the responses into two basic categories, death-affirming responses and death-denying responses.

A brief walk through a study of death rituals brings forth many questions. How does a death-affirming society, in contrast with a death-denying culture, deal with the problems of life, aging and death? How does the Euro-American feeling death's cold hands on the back of his neck deal with the inevitable compared to responses of ancient religions like Buddhism, Taoism, or Confucianism? What about traditional people who worshipped nature or ancestral spirits like the early Eskimos or American Indians? What prompted the Egyptians of long ago as well as some Asian cultures to bury live slaves and wives, as well as weapons and food, with their dead? Why do some Tswana tribes in South Africa bury the deceased under the floors of their houses? Why do some Chinese and the Basutoland tribesmen make a hole in the roof of their houses when someone passes on?

The questions continue. Why do some groups have wakes, stage banquets, perform dances, or wear black or white? Why do some destroy, dismember, drown, cremate, or bury the remains? Why do others preserve or beautify the corpse? As primitive or as exotic as some of these practices may appear to us, they not only reflect the way various cultures see life and death, but they also attest to the importance people attach to the death event. Whatever their rites and customs, social groups have often gone beyond the minimum procedures necessary to dispose of their departed. Pre-burial and post-burial rituals for the deceased generally reflect a whole cultural complex and an outlook on life and just as importantly serve a need for the living. They are perceived as a significant rite of passage ushering those who have passed on to the land of their forefathers.

The personal responses of the survivors continue the variations. On the one hand, society may discourage heart wrenching wailing or painful self-laceration that could prove debilitating to those grieving. On the other hand, such actions release tension and sorrow when the dreaded event occurs and helps them come to grips with the reality and finality of what has happened. These actions can assist those left behind with their own death issues, their guilt feelings, and their ambivalence toward the departed and his or her leaving them behind. If these actions are performed in a group setting, they may also serve a social purpose in bringing the families together again after their unity has been shaken by the event.

A resounding clash of cultures occurs when the dominant society inflicts its mores about death onto the lesser groups in its midst. Often it is oppressive, disrespectful, and even at times cruel. Just one of many examples of this happening occurred in the winter of the late 1800's at Wounded Knee, SD. A small band of Sioux Indians were camped under a flag of truce. The U.S. Cavalry, fearful of a possible uprising, mercilessly killed every man, woman, and child on the site then forced other Natives to hack out a long common grave in the snow-covered ground. The frozen bodies of the dead were thrown into the opening "like stacks of cordwood". This was especially heinous because the culturally acceptable way the Sioux and many Plains Indians in those days dealt with the cadavers was to place them on a platform face up, with honor and ceremony. They believed that placing a body face down meant the deceased would never find the road to the land of his ancestors and be forever damned to wander the earth in torment.

As implied by the cultural groups mentioned above *We-CHA-tah-pe* (Sioux for 'death') was dealt with by American Indians in various fashions. The mound builders of the upper Midwest had ceremonies, strangely similar to the Egyptians except for the mummification process, which was not at all uncommon in other Western Hemisphere Native cultures. Some of the many Eastern Woodlands tribes put their deceased in reed blankets before burial while others placed the bodies in high places, in the forest, in lakes or rivers, or even in caves. In the traditional Eskimo culture of the far north there are stories of an elder realizing death is at hand wandering away from the community to die so his or her remains will feed animals hunted by the village. Some Native American tribes were calloused toward the cadavers of their Indian or White enemies, defiling, scalping, decapitating, or even cannibalizing them. The heart was considered the source of an enemy's power and some removed it from the body. As a result of the Euro-American overrunning of this continent and the organized religions that followed, contemporary American Indians deal with their dead similar to their White counterparts. Often it includes an interment rite and burial, often Christian, followed by an Indian-culture wake. Maybe they are being sure they are covering all the bases.

* * * * * * * * *

So what are the ethics of death for North Americans of the twenty-first century? Are they death-affirming or death-denying? One way to look at this is to review the writings of Elisabeth Kubler-Ross and Ashley Miller as they present the six stages of grief:

1. Shock
2. Denial
3. Anger
4. Bargaining
5. Depression
6. Acceptance

Shock - Shock is the initial reaction to a loss, whether it is death, divorce, or any other form of misfortune that impacts an individual's functioning. Shock is the reaction that emerges out of a feeling of disbelief, leaving a sense of being temporarily numb. It is a defense mechanism that serves to protect the individual from being overwhelmed. This phase can last anywhere from a few days to a few weeks, depending on the gravity of the loss.

Denial - Denial is a defense mechanism that the individual employs when he or she is unwilling to accept the fact that the shocking event actually happened, whether the loss is finding out about the death of a loved one or finding out very bad news, such as learning that someone has a serious illness. The individual acts as though nothing has happened or refuses to accept that what he or she has heard is actually true.

In effect, he or she closes their minds to what has occurred and continues life for a certain length of time, acting as though nothing has changed.

Anger - Anger may occur at any point during the grieving process but typically it follows denial. Anger may be directed inward or outward, at others, at a specific person, or at society in general. In this phase, emotions that may have been pent up for quite some time tend to erupt and the frustration at having little or no control over circumstances may be directed toward anyone who gets in the way.

Bargaining - Bargaining is a heartfelt form of desperation in which the individual tries to make deals to regain what has been lost. The bereaved may negotiate with God or even with himself in order to reclaim a loved one. In this stage, people try their best to cling to what has been lost, even though they know it will never return.

Depression - When the individual accepts the inevitable and realizes that any efforts of avoidance are futile, a period of depression generally sets in. The realization that a person has no control over preventing any outcomes or changing anything causes the aggrieved to turn away from any support group, believing that there is no one who can understand their sense of loss or can help make things better. They build walls around themselves and may need professional help to break free.

Acceptance - Acceptance occurs when people learn to deal with the reality of the situation. They have walked through some or all of the previous phases of grief and they now move on to this final phase where they take action to get closure with what has happened or with what is going to happen. A sense of peace begins to present itself and the sufferer can approach the future with a more positive attitude.

May I offer a seventh stage of grief: "Anniversary depression." I first experienced this when my grandfather died during the Christmas season. For the next two or three years I just didn't seem to enjoy Christmas as much as I had before. I missed my grandfather and the season was special for both of us. Sometime later when I was a school principal I had a wonderful teacher working for me from Hawaii. She lost her father and the next year at the time of her loss she was so depressed I decided she should take a couple days off. The following year at that date we made plans for her to have a substitute teacher take over her classroom so she could grieve in privacy. This went on for a couple more years then she let me know it wasn't needed anymore. A recent example of "anniversary depression" occurred when my ex-wife died of cancer caused by the "down-winder syndrome" from the Hanford Atomic Energy Reservation in the southeastern section of the state of Washington. It has been a few years now but my youngest daughter still feels "blue" and tries to avoid social interactions on the date of her mother's death.

We, as adults, interfere with this logical process toward the inevitable when we shield the children from the fact of death, "Uncle Jim moved to California" or "Your kitty found a new friend and they are playing in his yard." We mask our own pain in their presence and often do not allow them to participate in the profundity of the death rites and rituals by using incorrect terms like "asleep" or "resting". I find it especially disconcerting when I go into a funeral room and see "the slumber room". In our ignorance we downplay or belittle the young one's feelings. We say things to them like "you're just a kid" or "you don't understand." Because of this, even though the purpose is to hide our personal pain from them, we do the children a terrible disservice. I remember when our old lady cat ate my daughter's hamster. She was five or six years old at that time. I told her that her pet had ran off to find a wife. Later in the day, she was sitting in her wagon at the edge of the lawn crying out, "Here hamster-hamster. Come home hamster-hamster." I felt terrible.

* * * * * * * * * *

Another Sweet Angel

Topher did not look good. He was pale and slim with dark rings under his sad eyes. When I would greet him with a gentle touch on his shoulder there was no snap of life that is noticeable in other children his age. This was Topher's first year in school, the most exciting time in a child's life and he moved like an old man, every motion seemed full of effort and clearly painful.

Topher was dying of leukemia. This sweet little boy had already placed his footsteps onto the pathway to diminishment and he was barely five years old. His classmates reached out to him and showed him a special fondness and affection even though they did not know nor understand what Topher was enduring. His mother said the most important thing in his life was to go to school one more day.

What could we do?

The Grim Reaper's cold mask followed him hungrily and this was especially magnified in an elementary school because the building is always full of life. There is no training manual for teachers that you can flip open and read "Death of a Child".

And what of the other children in his school life? How does one explain to them when the time comes? You can't honestly say, "Topher moved to California along with George the hamster."

His parents had a birthday party for him and invited all his classmates. He was heavily medicated to combat the agonizing pain, but his eyes glistened like Christmas tree lights. How incongruous this vision, bright eyes, dwindled body, colorful party hats, and happy music. The weight of reality shadowing the festivities.

Topher was not in his seat the following Monday morning. His empty little chair said so much without a word being spoken. In my role as the principal I was charged with telling the children he had died over the weekend. I entered the classroom and watched them quietly cutting and pasting at their tables. His classmates somehow sensed what had happened even though they had not been told.

They were quietly talking about Topher. In trust and acceptance, they were comforting and assuring each other that he was in heaven with God and not in pain anymore and that everything was okay now. In a wondrous wisdom they had accepted death as a normal part of life and were getting on with their day. The teacher and I shared a brief glance through teary eyes. She smiled and nodded. I too got into my day.

A classroom full of five year olds taught me a lesson I have never forgotten.

* * * * * * * *

American Indian Death Song

So if the deceased could talk to us, what would they say? I think it would be a hope for peace for the ones they loved. Consider this Native American Death Song:

> *Do not stand at my grave and weep.*
> *I am not there – I am not asleep.*
> *I am the cooling winds that blow.*
> *I am the gently falling snow.*
> *I am the whispering showers of rain.*
> *I am the memories of lonely pain.*
> *I am the warming sun on grasses' dew.*
> *I am the arms of love that caress you.*
> *I am with the birds in circling flight.*
> *I am the shine of stars on a clear night.*
> *Do not stand at my grave and cry.*
> *I am not there ... I did not die.*

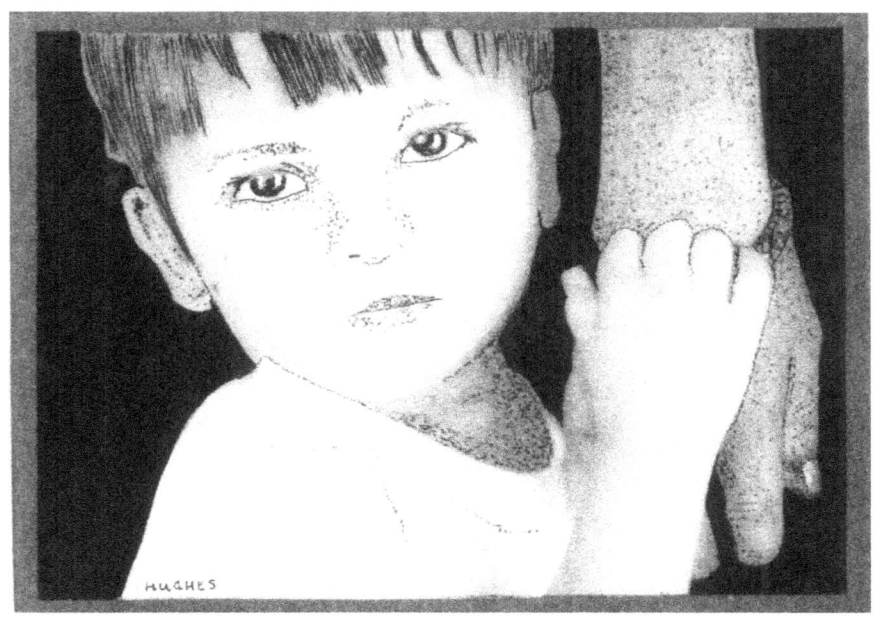

OUR HOPE FOR PEACE –
EMBRACING THE DISCONNECTED

Broken Children

My daughter was a para-professional for a number of years in the public school's most difficult class setting, the high school Behavioral Intervention program.

Wandering directionless through a number of years of public school, her students became unable or unwilling to fit into normal school life and ended up cloistered away as a last ditch effort to further their educations before they ended up on the streets or incarcerated. Broken in their own individual ways, they brought a burden of baggage so heavy it reflected in their eyes and their social interactions. Too many were in and out of juvenile detention and/or foster homes with really no sense of family or solid ground to place their feet as they were rapidly reaching adulthood. No love, no consistency, no future. My daughter told me one time that a young man in her classroom was wearing two ankle bracelets from the authorities. She perused his Facebook page and in every photo he was brandishing a firearm.

Some of their most severe issues reflected my growing up years and my daughter asked me to come and talk to them in the role of someone who had experienced what they were enduring and somehow had still "made it" in society. This was not going to be easy as I could feel old wounds starting to break open from memories I had hidden away for many years.

I began to develop an outline for my presentation and decided to offer it to the students as questions:

Who am I?
Why am I even in this life?
What is going to happen to me?
When will this emptiness go away?
Honestly, who really cares anyway?

As we talked about the issues, it became clear I had touched some very tender places. I told them that when I was a small child all I wanted was someone to cover me up on those cold nights when the blankets were on the floor. Night after night I laid there hoping. Then at some point I realized I had to do it myself and this became my bottom line message to the students. If they are waiting for someone to ease their pain and comfort their sorrows, "it just ain't gonna happen." Each of us needs to take responsibility for our own feelings and our own future. I was careful not to imply in any way that it would be easy, but with this mindset doors will open that had always been closed in our faces.

* * * * * * * * * *

It is human nature for all people to think they are safe and fear-free when they feel attached to their world and the people around them. Disconnected people are driven by anxiety and isolation so they endeavor to control their environment by using methods that often serve to widen the gap between them and the others in their lives. Spiritually and emotionally they become numb with walled off feelings that are more often physically expressed than verbally expressed. This common trait manifests itself by a general unwillingness to acknowledge pain in others and to not accept ownership for causing that pain.

Wherever they look, the disconnected see closed doors so they begin to believe they are completely unlovable and so they react by being un-loving. If they have a semblance of control in their lives, most of their energy is directed toward self-gratification regardless of the consequences crashing around them. If they do find themselves in trouble, they blame "the system", others, or claim "the devil made me do it." They are not motivated to set long-term or even short-term goals so there is little or no regard to what may happen next to them.

How the disconnected stumble into a situation like this is complicated and usually multifaceted that begins at an early age and continues onward. They are unable or unwilling to deal in socially acceptable ways with the feelings of anxiety, frustration, and rage that they are living with so they endeavor to control their lives and the people in them by ways they witnessed others doing to them and to the people they at one time cared about. Lacking knowledge of the choices actually available, they are in a reactionary phase that often involves bullying, hurting others, and domineering the meek and the weak.

Because of a lack of trust in people they often misperceive the motives of others. This gives them license to continually test the boundaries and push people away until those trying to help turn their backs. This reinforces their original feelings that they are unworthy of being loved and cared for.

Now you know how tough the problem is when you try to embrace the disconnected. Are there any strategies that have proven successful to some degree? A very important aspect is to provide an atmosphere that models acceptance and more importantly patience. Some of the characteristics of that setting include:

1. Establish a location that provides personal and emotional safety for all participants.
2. Remind them they must take responsibility for the resolution of their own problems.
3. Teach them, then model, goal-setting strategies. A very effective system is the "Person Center Planning" program.
4. Endeavor to reassure them that the "real" world out there is not necessarily all cruel and frantic. Many, many people are doing okay and it is not impossible for the disconnected to become part of that group
5. Display an attitude that models the good side of humanity and remember the importance of patience. Rome wasn't built in a day and bringing the disconnected back into the fold will take time and perseverance.
6. Stay positive and respectful. Questioning techniques should elicit participation from the subjects and should be equitable and uplifting rather than blaming.
7. Use your words rather than actions. Then work on the improvement of the use of language. Too many of the disconnected do not possess the vocabulary to actually express themselves, so they resort to profanity and threatening verbiage.
8. Establish some acceptable ground rules and boundaries that the participants are willing to agree to. The overall context of the sessions should be directed toward improving relationships in general.

9. A very difficult process involved is demonstrating and teaching ways that the participants can redirect their anger and frustration into more acceptable pathways. Admit you do not have all the answers but you are willing to share a few ideas that have worked for you.

10. Let them know you believe the disconnected can change for the better and endeavor to equip them with the techniques to do so.

11. Baby steps! If you are aware of even the tiniest bit of improvement, reinforce it.

12. Do not let a forceful participant wrest the person-in-charge role from you during the dialog or allow them to dominate the discussion.

There is another aspect of this situation that is far and away the most difficult and risky to address, embracing the spiritual nature of the participants. In general, the disconnected are unwilling to acknowledge they even have a spiritual side. So wrapped up in trying to survive in today's world, the deeper and tender part of people's lives are pushed so far down their cries for acceptance and appreciation fall on deaf ears. What can we do about it? About all we can do is share our attitudes and beliefs in a sincere and open fashion and hope modeling this will somehow open the hearts and minds of those we are working with. Here are some things to talk about.

1. Let each one know that you can see the light of God in their eyes. Tell them you believe that every person is put here to be a blessing and it is just a matter of helping them find out how to meet this responsibility. It was not some cosmic accident that they are walking on this needy planet.

2. Remind them that you believe that each person has been given a special gift to share with humanity, something they can do better than anybody else.

3. If you believe this, tell them that we all have the greatest mother of all, Mother Earth. She has a special love for those who feel like orphans because they have been abandoned by their human families. All they have to do is find a quiet place to lie down in a grassy field and relax. They will sense her warm arms embracing them and will feel her moist tears of sadness on their clothing. Some call it "dew".

4. Try to get them to see the "big picture". Remind them that they stand on a life continuum and are an important part of the process. They will be parents, grandparents, and ancestors. Those who follow will look back on them so it is important that they do so with appreciation and respect. The decisions the disconnected are making now will affect future generations not just themselves.

5. And most important of all, try to instill in the people feeling disenfranchised and forgotten that we are never really alone. Our world is full of life and joy that is waiting for each of us to take a sip. There are many people out there who really care. Give them a chance to find you.

OUR HOPE FOR PEACE – CANTICLE OF RECONCILIATION

The ground shaking under your feet is not an earthquake. It is our beautiful country being torn apart by a massive canyon promulgated by people, institutions, and government that is growing deeper and deeper every day because of the widening gap between those Americans who have "made it" and those who feel left out and beaten down. Simply stated, the rich are getting richer and the poor are falling further and further behind.

Can you not hear them crying out?

Listen as their pleas for fairness are swept away like fallen leaves in a wind storm:

Must different imply deficient? If my skin color is different from yours and my language is not as beautiful as yours, does that mean I am stupid or just incompetent? If I take a chance and try to communicate to you what is in my heart and endeavor to show you a glimpse of my soul, must you be so critical and judgmental? If tears of frustration fill my eyes, why do you turn away? Don't we all have the right to cry? Why are your hands over your ears? Why don't you answer me?

I am like you in more ways than you might want to consider. My justice agenda is your justice agenda. I am worthy of the fruits of a fair and sustainable American society. I implore you for access to education and health care and a promising future for myself, my children, and their children. Please allow me to access the minds and hearts of those of you in position to help me. I know they are there if you would only open the door. Are not the rights and freedoms that you enjoy for ALL Americans? Mr. Everyman, tear down that economic, spiritual, and actual wall you have built, and are continuing to build, to keep me out.

I ask you for the opportunity for self-determination. Provide me with the resources to make those decisions that affect my life. Neither institutions nor others can really know what I need. Allow me to enjoy the successes I have earned and allow me to grow from the mistakes I am bound to make. I am not asking for a handout, but I could use a hand now and then.

* * * * * * * * * *

In general, people of color and people of religions that differ from the Euro-American ethic have suffered, and suffer still, from vertical oppression. They are pressed down and held there. Small wonder they are fighting to get back to the surface, if just to be able to breathe. This is compounded by a phenomenon called "horizontal oppression". Within the communities mentioned above there is clearly hostile competition between brothers and sisters for finite resources, governmental services, jobs, education, housing, and health care. The irony is they are as unkind and as thoughtless to each other as the dominant society is to them. One very obvious reaction to this issue is the development of gangs and ghettos. The oppressed seek solace in the company of those experiencing similar circumstances for protection and a sense of identity.

These marvelous Americans trying to swim into the mainstream have found voices crying in the wilderness, endeavoring to bring their plight to the decision makers and attempting to open up the hearts of the people who look down on them. The high and mighty people do not like having a mirror held up to them showing how unwilling to compromise they have become, so they stop at nothing to silence the people touching their conscience. Our history is fraught with violence against the prophets of the needy. It is shameful.

So, how can we all make things better? The answer begins with a serious and heartfelt effort for reconciliation. The dictionary defines reconciliation as, "bringing back into friendship, adjusting, settling, and/or harmonizing". All of us must be willing to participate in this effort whether or not we have actually harmed someone with deeds done or undone. Here are the steps lying before us.

1. Take responsibility, without excuse, for what we have done or not done.
2. Approach the aggrieved in humility. Leave our pride at the front door.
3. Accept accountability for our actions and if we owe someone, pay up.
4. Make a personal commitment that the hurtful things we might have done are over.
5. Realize that people may question our honesty when we make reconciliation efforts and remember to put our words into action.

6. Understand that despite our sincerity some people are not ready to accept what we are trying to do. Too many have been beat down by unmet promises and hopeless expectations. They need time, so don't give up.

Only six steps? Sounds relatively easy to bring about. However, there are many reasons why reconciliation does not become a reality. As we stumble through life we might not realize that we have actually harmed people by our actions done or not done. Also, too many of us are fearful of those we do not understand and we are most comfortable in our ignorance of them and their issues. We want them to just go away. The reconciliation process takes hard work and determination and we just might not be able to give it a try. Each of us has a finite amount of energy to muster toward everyday living and endeavoring to meet the expectations placed on us by work, friends, family, and our nation. When we finally find some "me time" we want it to actually be "me time" at the expense of those around us. Help the needy? I promise to get around to it tomorrow.

At last, you ask the important question, "what can I do to reconcile with the downtrodden and disenfranchised in my community?"

There are many reputable organizations providing needed help and resources to those less fortunate. Determine some of those that appeal to you because of their work and commit a monetary donation on a regular basis to their cause. Become personally involved with a specific cultural group. Set aside your fears of the unknown and attend the religious ceremonies and cultural activities where everyone is invited. If a group in your community is planning a demonstration or sit-in for some cause, show up and carry a sign. Many cities have community centers where local people congregate for meals and activities, contact one that might be of interest to you and ask if you can volunteer in any capacity. Public schools in the barrios and ghettos can always use tutors to work with children needing a little help. This might prove to be a way to actually meet a family and get to know them. Many community colleges offer classes on minorities and different cultures. Sign up and get some "book learnin'". The dance is an important aspect of people across the globe and many have dance teams that give performances. Attend some of them and endeavor to mingle with the dancers after the shows, displaying a true interest in their culture and their needs. As you become known and accepted you will find closed doors beginning to open and you will be amazingly enriched by the new experiences.

OUR HOPE FOR PEACE –
GOD'S PROMISE OF A REMNANT

Thus says Yahweh:
At the favorable time I will answer you,
on the day of salvation I will help you.
(I have formed you and have appointed you
as covenant of the people.)
I will restore the land
and assign you the estates that lie waste.

I will say to the prisoners, "Come out."
To those who are in darkness, "Show yourselves".

They will never hunger or thirst,
scorching wind and sun shall never plague them;
For he who pities them will lead them
and guide them to springs of water.

...Shout for joy, you heavens; exult, you earth!
                    Isaiah 49:8-13
                    The Jerusalem Bible

The many *diaspora* of the Israelites brought a historically strong and oft-blessed people repeatedly to its knees. The "Land of Milk and Honey" slipped from their grasps and they became homeless and wretched. The Bible's Old Testament prophets tell us of their trials and persecution but intertwined through this entire theme is God's promise of a remnant.

No matter how stiff-necked and reticent the Israelites became nor how hopeless the situation, the Creator did not *entirely* erase His "Chosen People". In the fullness of time a "remnant", a small group of people, survived to provide the seed for the re-emergence of the children of Abraham.

Immersed in the lamentations of those difficult times, it must have been grinding agony for the families as well as the spiritual and political leaders to see their numbers dwindle away through war, starvation, and bitter deprivation. The people who once knew power, independence, and freedom found themselves facing hopelessness. They must have thought that God had turned His face from them and forgotten their name.

"My God, why hast thou forsaken me?"

Does history continue to repeat itself?

What about the American Indian? What about the United States in the twenty-first century?

One of my favorite books is George Wharton James' *Indian Basketry*. I have the 1909 fourth edition in my library. I was not so much interested in the baskets he found as I was in his accounting of the people he visited and how he was able to locate them in the wild mountainous country of northeastern California and southcentral Oregon. During the late 1800's, he traveled much of the area by train, horseback, and on-foot seeking out Indian villages, many of which were isolated and basically untouched by the Euro-American culture. He interviewed the people he found and collected baskets and other artifacts.

As I read his exploits I had to ask myself, *what happened to all of those villages and tribes? Is this just a small sampling of the North American version of the ten lost tribes of Israel?*

Some years ago a Native friend and I climbed a high mountain above Klamath Lake in southern Oregon to pray and chant the names of the Lost Tribes in that region. Please say them out loud.

Modok … Tolowa … Patawat … Wiyot … Mattoal … Lolonkuh … Wailakki… Yuki … Tatu … Poma … Yakaia … Gallinuomer …Wappo … Kabiapek … Makhelchel … Patwin … Wintun … Shastika … Maidu … Miwok … Paiuti …Yokut … Takelma … Tututni … Achumawi … Atsugewi … Yana … Kalapuya … Yaki …

In a geographical area not that much larger in size than Israel, twenty-nine tribes no longer walk this fair earth. The sense of loss overwhelmed me as these strangely beautiful names rolled over my tongue and out into the moonlit night. I wondered how long it had been since those names had been spoken. I wondered how this tragedy magnified itself across the entire North American continent.

My Native name, *Ha-Gue-A-Dees-Sas*, is Seneca for "Man Seeking His People." It was gifted to me by a traditional Indian Medicine Man after years of endeavoring to learn to walk on the pathway to Native American Spirituality consummated by a seven-day, water-only fast and vision quest in the Big Horn Mountains of Wyoming. Since then, I have traveled from coast to coast as well as Alaska, Hawaii, Canada, Mexico, and the Caribbean, "seeking my people." As the years passed it has become more and more clear I would be spending more time "seeking" than "finding".

In an indescribable way I experienced a sort of epiphany that maybe I should stop looking outward for "my people" and look inward. I guess I was trying to discover some sense of a remnant that would be applicable to me personally. My daughter found out that through my mother's father we were direct descendants of Chief Taptico of the Wicocomico people who lived in present day Virginia. History says that "… after June 1719 and the death of William Taptico, the English took the land, the 'remnants' of the Wicocomico dispersed and the tribe has been considered extinct."

My grandmother's people were the Kaskaskia clan of the Illinois Nation. In 1790, an effort was made by the United States government to take a census to determine how formidable the Illinois tribes might be as the Euro-Americans moved westward. They were a proud nation of horse riders and nomads and refused to stand still to be counted. They roamed from what is now Minnesota to Arkansas. The last of the Illinois Nation was herded onto the Winnebago Reservation of eastern Nebraska in 1870. A census count recorded a total of 161 people, mainly the elderly, women, and children. The Illinois are gone. The Kaskaskia are also considered extinct. At one time they had a small reservation west of Murphysboro, Illinois which is described as "now almost forgotten". There is an additional sense of irony because there is still a town in Illinois called Kaskaskia. The 2010 census listed fourteen people living there, none of whom are Native American.

Does God's promise of a remnant ring true also for the American Indian? It does not appear to be so. Maybe we might be willing to re-think the concept of a "remnant". Consider the following premises.

Premise 1: Little Sammie Jo and 'Big' Stan

Aunt Mick was an elegant woman who possessed some of the physical characteristics of her Cherokee heritage. She often spoke with pride of her blood line, but she did not look noticeably different from her Euro-American counterparts. Then along came grandchild Sammie Jo with flawless brown skin, coal-black eyes and hair, and the nose and facial structure of a full-blooded American Indian.

"She's a throwback," they explained.

"Big" Stan, my father, was called "Si-wash" by his classmates during his growing up years. This still is a hurtful derogatory term as insensitive as the N-word and means "half-breed". He considered himself an *ah-oh-ZE* of the Blackfoot Nation of the northcentral Great Plains. Grandmother said we were "French Canadians" when I asked her once if we were Indians. During his long life he called himself a "throwback" and blended successfully in any Native culture.

It has been determined that the American Indian gene is recessive. In any Indian inter-racial union whether White, Black, or Hispanic, the other ethnic characteristics dominate. Consider this thought, might this be Creator God's way of 'saving a remnant' for some future purpose? Could this be the manifesting of His plan to preserve 'His Chosen People' by hiding them within the gene pool of the dominant societies? In His wisdom he allows an occasional "throwback" to emerge now and then to provide hope for those grieving the loss of the Indigenous People of this continent.

Premise 2: A Reunification of the 'Remnants'

My mentor, Medicine Grizzly Bear, professes that "the families are getting together". After many centuries of Native Americans enduring their own *diaspora* across this vast land manifested by the creation of reservations and a Holocaust-like attitude toward the indigenous population, he is confident that the children are finding each other. Some primordial urge is causing genetic and spiritual family members to gravitate back together again.

For hundreds of years the original people who walked this land were torn and shredded then cast to the winds by incursions, economics, prejudice, and governmental actions. Now the mobility of American society and the availability of social media has allowed these threads to re-unite with each other and a remnant is forming once more. Unseen shepherd hands are gently pushing and herding the scattered flock. Grizzly Bear feels we are approaching the end times for our great nation and the re-weaving of the remnant is for survival as the tribulation races toward us.

Personally, I feel this phenomenon of reunification does not necessarily have to imply such a morbid purpose. Creator God has promised to rekindle His father-child relationship as mentioned in the Book of Isaiah and elsewhere and that the children, once more, may claim their "Promised Land". In this light, it is believable that the emerging of the remnant could be the beginning of newness and hope.

* * * * * * * * * * *

Again, the on-going question, does history repeat itself? Is there any way the promise of a remnant might apply to America?

These modern times seem especially critical to us as a nation. Have we become a stiff-necked and reticent people, silhouettes of the Israelites of days of old? We were a beacon of power, independence, and freedom for the world. Is this still true? Have we become self-centered and prejudiced against anybody who disagrees with us or looks or worships differently? Have these actions been modeled and validated by our political and social leadership? It seems we have been at war with ourselves or with others in some capacity or another for as long as our nation has existed. To complicate the issue, we have lived most of our lives under the threat of annihilation. I can remember as a school-aged child the "duck and cover" drills in preparation for the Russians dropping nuclear bombs on our cities. As that threat seemed to wane over the years, it was replaced by new fears and trepidations.

Now, the situation is even more exacerbated by a schism in our country between the wealthy and the needy that is growing wider than the Grand Canyon and seems to be getting deeper almost daily. A barely repressed anger and distrust in our government and the powerful who influence it seems to be just minutes away from revolution. At one time America was the moral compass for the world, demonstrating what is best in people personally and as a nation. Freedom, justice, and equality were not just words in a dictionary. We professed to be a godly nation and manifested this by printing "In God We Trust" on our currency and adding "Under God" to our Pledge of Allegiance. Other nations looked at us with respect and validation and many endeavored to emulate the points that made us great. Still other nations continue to look at us with jealousy and enmity.

Is my mentor and trainer Grizzly Bear correct? Are we approaching the end times for our nation? Will a remnant emerge from the rubble to reestablish our marvelous country? Whether the threat is from within or without, what is to become of us?

WHY A DOVE

God's promise of unconditional love
Kisses the world on the wings of a dove.

Why a dove?

With powerful eagles at His command,
Raptor and ravens always at hand.
Canadian geese around by the dozens.
Condors and owls and all their cousins.

Why a dove?

She is so fragile, a leaf in a storm.
Yet God's mighty words take temporal form
In a creature so small we don't even see.
A harbinger sent to find you and me.

Why a dove?

A still small voice brings a message of hope.
A friend in the night to help us to cope
With sadness and pain that darkens our door
She guides us back home to His holy shore.

That's why a dove.

INTROSPECTION

Olive Branches was written in an effort to shine some light on the darkness in our world. Peace in our time will be difficult to obtain and it has been this way since the very beginning as our great nation continues to strive to become a beacon of hope for all people.

So, what have we learned?

The planet Earth is not an endless bounty for people to harvest. More and more people are struggling for finite resources. Our nation continues to experience growing pains as the population wanders past 300 million people. There is a vast and growing canyon between those who enjoy more than enough and those who don't know from day to day if they will even survive. We can do our part by "living simply, so people can simply live". Our angst is compounded by those who express the concept of global warming. If the prognosticators are correct, we are in for continued weather related misfortunes.

Childhood is an exciting as well as a frightening time for our kids. A glimpse into their marvelous world will help us understand what they are going through. What children will become as adults begins to manifest itself as they venture through a school system. They need our support, our understanding, our patience and, yes, our prayers to improve their chances of becoming honest and productive citizens.

Each of us needs a quiet place to recharge our batteries and gather the strength to carry on. You owe it to yourself to step back and look at where your life is leading you. Somebody or something will greedily take every minute of your time. Be strong enough to say "whoa!" As you seek your refuge you may be lucky enough to find your *watai* (special stone) to keep you company. Hide it in your pocket or your purse. It belongs to nobody but YOU!

Our communities of faith, regardless of rite and ritual, are not stagnant and sedentary. WE must be vigilant toward the hell worms that burrow from without and from within to decay what we hold dear. We need to continually renew our commitment and energies to guarantee the survival of our heartfelt beliefs. Each of us must become warriors willing to sacrifice for the good of all without the fear of prejudice, reprisal, or even death.

Do you live in a death-affirming or death-denying culture? Even more importantly, how do YOU feel about this? Each of us is the finished product of the impact the act of death has on our families, our religion, our friends, and our society. Consider the idea held by traditional Native people that death is one aspect of the Circle of Life, no more or less important than the rest of the Circle. When you think about it, it is a rather healthy perspective. In all situations and beliefs the death of the body is inevitable. Have you taken the time to ask what happens next?

Too many of our brothers and sisters have been forgotten. They stand unfulfilled, empty and, directionless. It is up to us to embrace them and bring them back to the fold regardless of our trepidations or perceived lack of knowing how. Hopefully, some of the strategies shared in the chapters "Embracing the Disconnected" and "Canticle of Reconciliation" will assist us as we endeavor to help.

No matter how bad things may become we rest in hope that our nation will survive to blossom and to reach for the stars. In this, we hold tightly onto our hope for peace.

The Promise of the Great Spirit

My Child, This advice you must heed.
Please never take more than you need.
Promise to do these things I say,
And I will care for you in every way.

In Spring, I'll make the grasses grow.
I'll sing to raise the Buffalo.
As Summer Walks the waking lands,
I'll pull the Roots with my own hands.

Red Berries sweet will paint the Fall.
The Deer will answer to my call.
When Winter comes, it will be mild.
These things I promise you, my Child.

Choose NOT to honor my request.
You'll always wander in your quest.
Seeking, not finding your true home.
Lost nomads, empty and alone.

TENEBRAE

Creator-God stood on the Mount and looked at all He made.
North-South-East-and West He felt His spirit fade.

His streams were poisoned and choked with trash.
His beautiful trees were piles of slash.

Green hills and dales, once happy places.
Now brooding towns with asphalt faces.

The smoking war machines rumbled on.
Killing and maiming from dusk to dawn.

Innocent children, orphaned and lost.
Their families destroyed so great the cost.

Where eagles flew, now vultures nested.
Bellies full, they lazily rested.

Gentle creatures groaned from hunger's bite.
Hiding in fear through the endless night.

So, who has survived to claim the prize?
The new rulers of the earth, the flies.

A sweep of His hand, He could make it right.
He can do wonders with His power and might.

But He just turned His back and walked away.

Ha-Gue-A-Dees-Sas

APPENDIX 1

A Look at an Indian Treaty

The tragic story of treaties made and treaties broken between the United States government and its Indian nations has been, and will always be, a glaring example of power and greed running rough-shod over an Indigenous People.

A treaty is defined as, "an agreement made by negotiation or diplomacy; specifically, an agreement, league, or contract, between two or more states or sovereigns, formally signed and usually ratified."

Indian treaties usually had a similar format:

a.   A list of the signatories in attendance.

b.   A description of the boundaries of the land ceded to the United States.

c. A geographical description of the remainder of the land "re-served" for the Indigenous People.
d. What the government would offer in return.
e. Restrictions and/or regulations placed on the tribes.
f. Effective dates of enactment of the treaty.
g. The actual signatures or marks of participants and witnesses.

Too often a group of tribes or bands would be umbrellaed under a treaty despite the fact that the only thing they had in common was geography. Ongoing and former grievances, conflicts, and degradations were not easily forgotten. This issue complicated the consummation of agreements and sometimes it took a saber to get the leaders to put their "X" on the treaty document. Many, many tribes and bands just disappeared from history as they were confederated under one label. The scribe recording the treaty Anglicized the names and spellings of the different groups which seldom rang true to what they or their neighbors called themselves. This was also the case with many European immigrants processed through Ellis Island during this time and later.

A typical example of a treaty might be the agreement written in 1855 and ratified in 1859 between the U.S. government and the Yakima Indian Nation of present-day Washington State. (See below for complete text of treaty).

The first Article of the treaty maps out the land that the Indians will:

"...*cede, relinquish, and convey to the United States...*"

This real estate is identified by topographical features and longitude and latitude. There is a strange irony about the description of this land considered by the U.S. government as "belonging" to the Yakama Nation. Traditional Indian people did not understand what it meant to "own" land. As far as they were concerned, Mother Earth belonged to the Creator and was a gift provided for the survival and sustenance of the two-leggeds. Terms like "cede", "claims", and "title" were not in their language and were simply not translatable. "Latitude" and "longitude" had no meaning to them at all and the geographic features mentioned in the boundary descriptions were usually the Euro-American names inscribed on very sketchy maps held by the territory government and military. Very few of the local Native names ever appeared on any treaty, so the Indians had no idea what the White Men were talking about. If the land described in the Yakima Treaty was truly "owned" by the Indians, and they had not been coerced into selling it, their present-day reservation would encompass the very heart of Washington State and have an irregular shape with the dimensions of 208 miles north and south and 176 miles east and west, rather than the current 1,377,034 acre, roughly trapezoidal shaped reservation forty miles by seventy-two miles.

The second Article describes the boundaries of the reservation itself. A proviso in this clause addresses the issue:

> "...any improvements heretofore made by the Indian, such as fields enclosed and cultivated, and houses erected upon the lands hereby ceded, and which he may be compelled to abandon in consequence of this treaty, shall be valued, under the direction of the President of the United States, and payment made..."

This article seems rather magnanimous toward the indigenous people until we realize that most of them did not cultivate the land, nor did they perform improvements on said property. The Plateau People of central Washington and Oregon were fishermen, hunters, and gatherers. Their lifestyle involved the ability to be very mobile and flexible.

The "White Man speaks with forked tongue" issue emerged almost instantly. Territorial Governor Stevens threw open Indian lands for white settlers less than two weeks after the treaty was signed. Chief Kamiakin called upon the tribes and bands to oppose the declaration. Some of the Natives joined forces under Kamiakin and managed to battle the U.S. soldiers for about three years in an uprising called The Yakima War (1855-1858). Colonel George Wright brutally defeated the Indians in the fall of 1858 southwest of the present city of Spokane, Washington. His troops confiscated hundreds of the native's horses and massacred them on the banks of the Spokane River near the present Washington-Idaho border believing that native people without horses cannot make war. Wright, unmoved by the Indians' grievances appointed himself judge and jury, apprehended two dozen of the Yakama leaders, and hung them in a pastoral valley south of Spokane called Hangman Creek. Word of his ruthlessness reached Kamiakin, who was able to escape to Canada. Wright's actions were so edified by the White majority that they named a large military installation after him that served as a training center during World War II and a women's college for some twenty years after that war.

Within a few months of the actual ratification of the treaty, an entire people was uprooted from its traditional hunting grounds, berry fields, and fishing locations and re-situated in a strange environment that those already living there had never had to share before. This proved to be an unbearable hardship for the displaced, as well as the settled, and forced many of them to rely on the U.S. government for sustenance and survival.

Article three provides for road building on reservation land and Indian access to government built roads off-reservation. During the time of the development of the treaty Indians were not considered American citizens and it was felt the road issue had to be addressed so the reservation inhabitants were not isolated to their own property.

The second part of this clause discusses Indian fishing rights. One small phrase from this Article has proven to be an incredible bone of contention that some feel still has not been resolved fairly, "...the right of taking fish at all usual and accustomed places..." In the 1850's, this really was not an important issue. There were plenty of salmon and steelhead, private land owners had not fenced off access to the fishing spots, the major dams on the Columbia River had not even been thought about, and a commercial and sports fishing economy was not putting pressure on the environment and the politicians. Starting with a court battle in 1905 (United States vs. Winans) there were over twenty adjudication cases, some of which went as far the United States Supreme Court. The bottom line emerged that the natives do not have unrestricted fishing rights off reservation despite the spirit of the treaty.

The fifth article reflects the values and ideals of the dominant society and was completely insensitive to the ages-old culture of the indigenous people. This clause was to provide money to build and equip two schools and a hospital. It also had a provision for the construction of a saw mill, flour mill, and various shops for a blacksmith, carpenter, wagon and plough maker, a tin smith, and a gunsmith. The Yakamas had survived and prospered for thousands of years without these accommodations and now they would have to be whittled down to fit into the new boxes. Their confinement to the reservation contributed to ill health, atrophy, alcoholism, and other problems such as tuberculosis, pneumonia, and gastrointestinal disorders. Infant mortality rates far exceeded those of the non-reservation population and heart disease, suicide, and diabetes became the leading causes of death among the Yakamas. The Indian boarding school on the reservation at Ft. Simco was not unlike any of the other institutions scattered across the West. The agenda was to educate the native children to become puzzle pieces in the overall picture of the Manifest Destiny of a melting pot United States. The price the young people paid was exacted from their culture, their language, and their family traditions.

Article 6 discusses the criteria for allotting reservation land and was instrumental in the inevitable demise of native property ownership, even on "Indian land." In the treaty with the Yakima, it refers the reader to prior rules laid out in the agreement with the Omaha Indians of the upper Midwest that was ratified the prior year. (See below). The point is that all the native signatories had no idea what was being talked about and probably most of the white men were in the same situation. The Omaha document lays out how much land each tribal member who is "...willing to avail themselves of the privilege..." of moving onto surveyed land is allotted. On every reservation, there was more land than the natives could occupy under those rules and regulations. The remaining un-surveyed land was sold or leased by the agency to white farmers and ranchers at pennies on the dollar. Even today, a plat map of many Indian reservations displaying land ownership looks like a multi-colored checker board. Some Indian Nations have developed a re-buying program to get back the reservation and off-reservation real estate that was originally theirs.

The final five Articles of the treaty delineate the expectations of the United States government on the Yakama people. Such terms as "promise to be friendly" and "agree not to shelter or conceal offenders against the laws of the United States" make it clear that there is no sovereignty even though the Indian-U.S. Government relationship is in treaty form. Most treaties have strict rules against the distilling, selling, or using ardent spirits on reservation land and the Yakima agreement is no exception. A reservation occupant found with alcohol "may have his or her annuities withheld from him or her for such time as the President may determine."

Many of the Articles imply that the President of the United States is directly involved in the decisions and the operations of the reservation. This implication added a certain amount of clout to the document in the eyes of the native signatories. The Great White Father image made the Indians feel that their concerns were noticed and were important to the most powerful leader of the White Men. In reality, this was far, far from true. There is no record of any U.S. President visiting an Indian reservation until well into the 1900's.

* * * * * * * *

Treaty with the Yakima 1855

Articles of agreement and convention made and concluded at the treaty-ground, Camp Stevens, Walla-Walla Valley, this ninth day of June, in the year one thousand eight hundred and fifty-five, by and between Isaac I. Stevens, governor and superintendent of Indian affairs for the Territory of Washington, on the part of the United States, and the undersigned head chiefs, chiefs, head-men, and delegates of the Yakama, Palouse, Pisquouse, Wenatshapam, Klikatat, Klinquit, Kow-was-say-ee, Li-ay-was, Skin-pah, Wish-ham, Shyiks, Oche-chotes, Kah milt-pah, and Se-ap-cat, confederated tribes and bands of Indians, occupying lands hereinafter bounded and described and lying in Washington Territory, who for the purposes of this treaty are to be considered as one nation, under the name of "Yakama" with Kamaiakun as its head chief, on behalf of and acting for said tribes and bands, and being duly authorized thereto by them.

ARTICLE 1. The aforesaid confederated tribes and bands of Indians hereby cede, relinquish, and convey to the United States all their right, title, and interest in and to the lands and country occupied and claimed by them, and bounded and described as follows, to wit:

Commencing at Mount Ranier (sp.), thence northerly along the main ridge of the Cascade Mountains to the point where the northern tributaries of Lake Che-lan and southern tributaries of the Methow

River have their rise: then southeasterly on the divide between the waters of Lake Che-lan and the Methow River to the Columbia River; then, crossing the Columbia on a true east course, to a point whose longitude is one hundred and nineteen degrees and ten minutes which two latter lines separate the above confederated tribes and bands from the Oakinakane tribe of Indians; thence in a true south course to the forty-seventh parallel of latitude; thence east on said parallel to the main Palouse River, which two latter lines of boundary separate the above confederated tribes and bands from the Spokanes; thence down the Palouse River to its junction with the Moh-hah-ne-she, or southern tributary of the same; thence in a southeasterly direction to the Snake River, at the mouth of the Tucannon River, separating the above confederated tribes from the Nez Perce' tribe of Indians; thence down the Snake River to its junction with the Columbia River; thence up the Columbia River to the "White Banks" below the Priest's Rapids; thence westerly to a lake called "La Lac"; thence southerly to a point on the Yakama River called Toh-mah-luke; thence, in a southwesterly direction to the Columbia River, at the western extremity of the "Big Island," between the mouths of the Umatilla River and Butler Creek; all which latter boundaries separate the above confederated tribes and bands from the Walla-Walla, Cayuse, and Umatilla Tribes and bands of Indians; thence down the Columbia River to midway between the mouths of the White Salmon and Wind Rivers; thence along the divide between said rivers to the main ridge of the Cascade Mountains; and thence along said ridge to the place of beginning.

ARTICLE 2. There is, however, reserved, from the lands above ceded for the use and occupation of the aforesaid confederated tribes and bands of Indians, the tract of land included within the following boundaries, to wit: Commencing on the Yakama River, at the mouth of the Attah-nam River; thence westerly along said Attah-nam River to the forks; thence along the southern tributary to the Cascade Mountains; thence southerly along the main ridge of said mountains, passing south and east of Mount Adams, to the spur whence flows the waters of the Klickatat and Pisco Rivers; thence down said spur to the divide between the waters of said rivers; thence along said divide to the divide separating the waters of the Satass River from those flowing into the Columbia River; thence along said divide to the main Yakama, eight miles below the mouth of the Satas River; and thence up the Yakama River to the place of beginning.

All which tract shall be set apart and, so far as necessary, surveyed and marked out, for the exclusive use and benefit of said confederated tribes and bands of Indians, as an Indian reservation; nor shall any white man, excepting those in the employment of the Indian Department, be permitted to reside upon the said reservation without permission of the tribe and the superintendent and agent. And the said confederated tribes and bands agree to remove to, and settle upon, the same, within one year after the ratification of this treaty. In the mean time it shall be lawful for them to reside upon any ground not in the actual claim and occupation of citizens of the United States; and upon any ground claimed or occupied, if with the permission of the owner or claimant.

Guaranteeing, however, the right to all citizens of the United States to enter upon and occupy as settlers any lands not actually occupied and cultivated by said Indians at this time, and not included in the reservation above named.

And provided that any substantial improvements heretofore made by any Indian, such as fields enclosed and cultivated, and houses erected upon the lands hereby ceded, and which he may be compelled to abandon in consequence of this treaty, shall be valued, under the direction of the President of the United States, and payment made therefore in money; or improvement of an equal value made for said Indian upon the reservation. And no Indian will be required to abandon the improvements aforesaid, now occupied by him, until their value in money, or improvements of an equal value shall be furnished him as aforesaid.

ARTICLE 3. And provided that, if necessary for the public convenience, roads may be run through the said reservation; and on the other hand, the right of way, with free access from the same to the nearest public highway, is secured to them; as also the right, in common with citizens of the United States, to travel upon all public highways.

The exclusive right of taking fish in all the streams, where running through or bordering said reservation, is further secured to said confederated tribes and bands of Indians, as also the right of taking fish at all usual and accustomed places, in common with the citizens of the Territory, and of erecting temporary buildings for curing them; together with the privilege of hunting, gathering roots and berries, and pasturing their horses and cattle upon open and unclaimed land.

ARTICLE 4. In consideration of the above cession, the United States agree to pay the said confederated tribes and bands of Indians, in addition to the goods and provisions distributed to them at the time of signing this treaty, the sum of two hundred thousand dollars, in the following manner, that is to say: sixty thousand dollars, to be expended under the direction of the President of the United States, the first year after the ratification of this treaty, in providing for their removal to the reservation, breaking up and fencing farms, building houses for them, supplying them with provisions and a suitable outfit, and for such other objects as he may deem necessary, and the remainder in annuities as follows. For the first five years after the ratification of the treaty, ten thousand dollars each year, commencing September first, 1856; for the next five years, eight thousand dollars each year; for the next five years, six thousand dollars per year; and for the next five years, four thousand dollars per year.

All which sums of money shall be applied to the use and benefit of said Indians, under the direction of the President of the United States, who may from time to time determine, at his discretion, upon what beneficial objects to expend the same for them. And the superintendent of Indian affairs, or other proper officer, shall each year inform the President of the wishes of the Indians in relation thereto.

ARTICLE 5. The United States further agree to establish at suitable points within said reservation, within one year after the ratification hereof, two schools, erecting the necessary buildings, keeping them in repair, and providing them with furniture, books, and stationery, one of which shall be an agricultural and industrial school, to be located at the agency, and to be free to the children of the said confederated tribes and bands of Indians, and to employ one superintendent of teaching and two teachers; to build two blacksmiths' shops, to one of which shall be attached a tin-shop, and to the other a gunsmith's shop, one carpenter's shop, one wagon and plough maker's shop, and to keep the same in repair and furnished with the necessary tools; to employ one superintendent of farming and two farmers, two blacksmiths, one tinner, one gunsmith, one carpenter, one wagon and plough maker, for the instruction of the Indians in trades and to assist them in the same; to erect one saw-mill and one flouring-mill, keeping the same in repair and furnished with the necessary tools and fixtures; to erect a hospital, keeping the same in repair and provided with the necessary medicines and furniture, and to employ a physician; and to erect, keep in repair, and provided with the necessary furniture, the building required for the accommodation of the said employees. The said buildings and establishments to be maintained and kept in repair as aforesaid, and the employees to be kept in service for the period of twenty years.

And in view of the fact that the head chief of the said confederated tribes and bands of Indians is expected, and will be called upon to perform many services of a public character, occupying much of his time, the United States further agree to pay to the said confederated tribes and bands of Indians five hundred dollars per year, for the term of twenty years after the ratification hereof, as a salary for such person as the said confederated tribes and bands of Indians may select to be their head chief, to build for him at a suitable point on the reservation a comfortable house, and properly furnish the same, and to plough and fence ten acres of land. The said salary to be paid to, and the said house to be occupied by, such head chief so long as he may continue to hold that office.

And it is distinctly understood and agreed that at the time of the conclusion of this treaty Kamaiakun is the duly elected and authorized head chief of the confederated tribes and bands aforesaid, styled the Yakama Nation, and is recognized as such by them and by the commissioners on the part of the United States holding this treaty; and all the expenditures and expenses contemplated in this article of this treaty shall be defrayed by the United States, and shall not be deducted from the annuities agreed to be paid to said confederated tribes and bands of Indians. Nor shall the cost of transporting the goods for the annuity payments be a charge upon the annuities, but shall be defrayed by the United States.

ARTICLE 6. The President may, from time to time, at his discretion, cause the whole or such portions of such reservation as he may think proper, to be surveyed into lots, and assign the same to such individuals or families of the said confederated tribes and bands of Indians as are willing to avail themselves of the privilege, and will locate on the same as a permanent home, on the same terms and subject to the same regulations as are provided in the sixth article of the treaty with the Omahas, so far as the same may be applicable.

ARTICLE 7. The annuities of the aforesaid confederated tribes and bands of Indians shall not be taken to pay the debts of individuals.

ARTICLE 8. The aforesaid confederated tribes and bands of Indians acknowledge their dependence upon the Government of the United States, and promise to be friendly with all citizens thereof, and pledge themselves to commit no depredations upon the property of such citizens.

And should any one or more of them violate this pledge, and the fact be satisfactorily proved before the agent, the property taken shall be returned, or in default thereof, or if injured or destroyed, compensation may be made by the Government out of the annuities.

Nor will they make war upon any other tribe, except in self-defense, but will submit all matters of difference between them and other Indians to the Government of the United States or its agent for decision, and abide thereby. And if any of the said Indians commit depredations on any other Indians within the Territory of Washington or Oregon, the same rule shall prevail as that provided in this article in case of depredations against citizens. And the said confederated tribes and bands of Indians agree not to shelter or conceal offenders against the laws of the United States, but to deliver them up to the authorities for trial.

ARTICLE 9. The said confederated tribes and bands of Indians desire to exclude from their reservation the use of ardent spirits, and to prevent their people from drinking the same, and, therefore, it is provided that any Indian belonging to said confederated tribes and bands of Indians, who is guilty of bringing liquor into said reservation, or who drinks liquor, may have his or her annuities withheld from him or her for such time as the President may determine.

ARTICLE 10. And provided, that there is also reserved and set apart from the lands ceded by this treaty, for the use and benefit of the aforesaid confederated tribes and bands, a tract of land not exceeding in quantity one township of six miles square, situated at the forks of the Pisquouse or Wenatshapam River, and known as the "Wenatshapam Fishery," which said reservation shall be surveyed and marked out whenever the President may direct, and be subject to the same provisions and restrictions as other Indian reservations.

ARTICLE 11. This treaty shall be obligatory upon the contracting parties as soon as the same shall be ratified by the President and Senate of the United States.

In testimony whereof, the said Isaac I. Stevens, governor and superintendent of Indian affairs for the Territory of Washington, and the undersigned head chief, chiefs, headmen, and delegates of the afore said confederated tribes and bands of Indians, have hereunto set their hands and seals, at the place and on the day and year herein before written.

Issac I. Stevens
Governor and Superintendent

Kamiakun (his x mark)   Wish-och-kmpits (his x mark)
Skloom (his x mark)   Koo-lat-toose (his x mark)
Owhi (his x mark)   Shee-ah-cotte (his x mark)
Te-cole-kun (his x mark)   Tuck-quille (his x mark)
La-hoom (his x mark)   Ka-loo-as (his x mark)
Me-ni-nock (his x mark)   Scha-noo-a (his x mark)
Elit Palmer (his x mark)   Sla-kish (his x mark)

Signed and sealed in the presence of –
 James Doty, secretary of treaties,
 Mie. Cles. Pandosy, O.M.T.,
 Wm. C. McKay,
 W.H. Tappan, sub Indian agent, W.T.,
 C. Chirouse, O.M.T.,
 Patrick McKenzie, interpreter,
 A.D. Pamburn, interpreter,
 Joel Palmer, superintendent of Indian affairs, O.T.,
 W.D. Biglow,
 A.D. Pamburn, interpreter. (listed twice for some reason)

Article 6 – Treaty with the Omahas
The President may, from time to time, at his discretion, cause the

whole or such portion of the land hereby reserved, as he may think proper, or of such other land as may be selected in lieu thereof, as provided for in article first, to be surveyed into lots, and to assign to such Indian or Indians of said tribe as are willing to avail of the privilege, and who will locate on the same as a permanent home, if a single person over twenty-one years of age, one-eighth of a section; to each family of two, one quarter section; to each family of three and not exceeding five, one half section; to each family of six and not exceeding then, one section; and to each family over ten in number, one quarter section for every additional five members. And he may prescribe such rules and regulations as will insure to the family, in case of the death of the head thereof, the possession and enjoyment of such permanent home and the improvements thereon. And the President may, at any time, in his discretion, after such person or family has made a location on the land assigned for a permanent home, issue a patent to such person or family for such assigned land, conditioned that the tract shall not be aliened or leased for a longer term than two years; and shall be exempt from levy, sale, or forfeiture, which conditions shall continue in force, until a State constitution, embracing such lands within its boundaries shall have been formed.

Appendix 2 - References

Borenstein, S. (October 2017) Monster Hurricanes Roiling Atlantic. *Associated Press Does the U.S. Have a Population Problem?* Facing the Future – People and the Planet. Retrieved from http://www.facingthefuture.org

Donne, J. (2002).*The American Heritage New Dictionary of Cultural Literacy* (3rd ed.). Boston, MA.: Houghton Mifflin Harcourt

Global Footprint Network. (2016), National Footprint Accounts. Retrieved from https://www.footprintnetwork.org/

Hurricanes. (2017) National Weather Service. Retrieved from https://www.nhc.noaa.gov/

Kubler-Ross, E. & Kessler, D. (1969). On Grief and Grieving: Finding the Meaning of Grief Through the Five Stages of Loss.

Miller, A. (2017, August 14). *The 6 Steps of Grieving.* Retrieved from https://www.livestrong.com/article/115001-six-steps-grieving/

CO2 Time Series 1990-2014 per Capita for World Countries. (2016). Netherland Environmental Assessment Agency.

State Farm Road Atlas. (1944). Rand McNally & Company.

U.S Census. *Population Clock: World.* www.census.gov/popclock/world. [Accessed Jan 2017].

Water Resources and Fisheries. (2004). World Resources Institute. Earth Trends Data Tables.

ABOUT THE AUTHOR

Stan Hughes aka *Ha-Gue-A-Dees-Sas* (Seneca for "Man seeking his people") is a retired public school administrator and university supervisor
with an extensive publication background, including an Editor's Choice
Award from the International Library of Poetry and a Silver Arrow
Award for Outstanding Contribution to Native American Literature
from Spirit Wind Records. He worked many years for the Indian Education Technical Assistance Center III at Gonzaga University in
Spokane, Washington. He was active in Indian education issues in both
the states of Washington and Oregon and he served on the board of
the Urban Indian Center in Spokane.

Although not enrolled in a federally recognized tribe, his grandparents were of Native American descent. His deceased father considered himself an *Ah-oh-ZE* (part-blood) of the Blackfoot Nation
located in north central Montana and southern Alberta, Canada.
Hughes was born on Yakama Indian land in Washington State
and grew up in the Black Hills of South Dakota, considered sacred
by the Sioux Nation. He is a Vietnam Era veteran and served in the
U.S. Army and U.S. Army Reserve from 1959 to 1965. He also was
a member of the United States intelligence community from 1966
to 1968.

Hughes was trained by traditional shamans (Medicine People) from
northern California and participated in a Rite of Passage to Warrior

Status during a seven-day, water-only fast and vision quest in the Big Horn Mountains of Wyoming.

The author has been a repeated guest on many internet radio programs and has been invited to speak at a number of conventions and gatherings from Alaska to Alabama. He has written two books on Native American topics, *Medicine Seeker – A Beginner's Walk on the Pathway to Native American Spirituality* and *Children of the Bluefish*.

www.ingramcontent.com/pod-product-compliance
Lightning Source LLC
Chambersburg PA
CBHW071354310526
45790CB00017B/381